Mainsail to the Wind

A Book of Sailing Quotations

Mainsail to the Wind

A Book of Sailing Quotations

Maryann —
Thanks for all the great
help you've given me at
Keyport over many happy
+ busy years! Fair winds
+ following seas.
Bill Galvani

William Galvani

S

SHERIDAN HOUSE

Special thanks and appreciation to my daughter
Stephanie L. Galvani for her assistance in preparing this book.

First published 1999 by
Sheridan House Inc.
145 Palisade Street
Dobbs Ferry, NY 10522

Library of Congress Cataloging-in-Publication Data

Mainsail to the wind: a book of sailing quotations/ [compiled by]
   William Galvani
      p.   cm
      Includes bibliographical references and index.
      ISBN 1-57409-069-0 (hc.:alk. paper). — ISBN 1-57409-067-4 (pbk.:
   alk. paper)
      1. Sailing Quotations, maxims, etc. I. Galvani, William.
   PN6084.S26M35   1999
   707.1'24—dc21   99-31027
                                          CIP

Editor: Janine Simon
Production Management: Quantum Publishing Services, LLC, Bellingham, WA
Composition/Design: Jill Mathews

Printed in the United States of America

ISBN   1-57409-069-0 (hardcover)
         1-57409-067-4 (paper)

*T*o my mother Helen who gave me a love of reading
and my father Amedeo who introduced me to the sea
and the ships that sail upon it.

Contents

Introduction

Mainsail to the Wind is about sailors, sailboats, and the sea. Marine engines and power-driven vessels do not intrude here.

I started reading about the sea in my teens, years before I first raised the mainsail in a sailboat. Over the past 30 years I have sailed when and where I could, always for enjoyment but never often enough. Reading about sailing sometimes had to substitute for the pleasure of the real thing.

About ten years ago I began to jot down sentences from my reading that seemed to me to distill the essence of life at sea. My notebooks grew to include almost 1,000 quotations from hundreds of sources, some as old as the Sumerian epic of Gilgamesh and others as recent as remarks made during the 1998 Whitbread Round the World Race. The sources included books, journals, poems, logs, chanteys, interviews, sayings, psalms, prayers, and more. They originated in the words and writings of 300 men and women. Most of the people quoted are sailors, but others are poets, scientists, journalists, explorers, and even a Roman emperor. For me, the quotes capture the activity, enjoyment, and tension of sailing and the sea.

I hope the quotations in *Mainsail to the Wind* will evoke your own memories of the sea and sailboats. I also hope these fragments of writing will encourage readers to obtain and read the complete works by the men and women whose original writings made this book possible. Sailing and reading are both voyages, and one makes the other better.

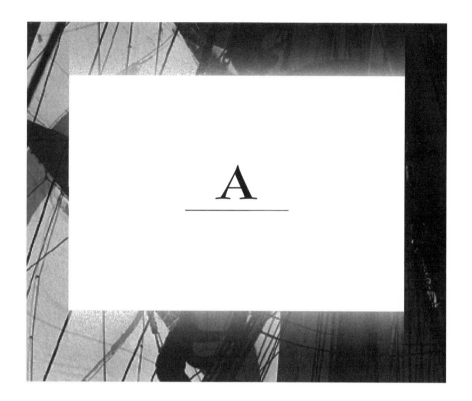

America's Cup

The eyes of the world are on you. You will be beaten, and the country will be abused...

> **HORACE GREELEY** to Captain Brown of the schooner *America* in France prior to the first race for the Hundred Guinea Cup, 1851

There is no second place, ma'am.

> Reply, probably apocryphal, to Queen Victoria when she inquired about the second finisher in the first race for the America's Cup, 1851

I think I'll have a shot at the old mug.

> **SIR THOMAS LIPTON** planning the first of his five unsuccessful attempts to win the America's Cup, 1898

Gentlemen, I shall be back.

> **SIR THOMAS LIPTON** after losing his first America's Cup series in 1899. He would lose four more series over the next 31 years.

For the sake of the sport I would like to see Sir Thomas win. As it is, the contest is too one-sided, but if the Cup passed and repassed across the ocean it would be better for yachting on both sides.

> **Editor of** *The Rudder,* an American yachting magazine, about Sir Thomas Lipton's second challenge for the America's Cup, 1901

I will not challenge again. I cannot win.

> **SIR THOMAS LIPTON** after his challenger *Shamrock V* was defeated in Lipton's fifth and last challenge for the America's Cup, 1930

Maybe you can make the darned thing go.

> **HAROLD 'MIKE' VANDERBILT** as he turned over the helm of *Rainbow* to Sherman Hoyt. *Rainbow* trailed the British yacht *Endeavour* by 6 minutes 39 seconds in the third race of the 1934 America's Cup series. Hoyt made up the deficit and won the race.

Britannia rules the waves, but America waives the rules.

> Unattributed quotation regarding a protest in the fourth race of the 1934 America's Cup. The U.S. defender *Rainbow*, sailed by Harold Vanderbilt, was involved in a luffing violation with Great Britain's *Endeavour*. Great Britain protested but the New York Yacht Club rejected the protest.

Protesting the New York Yacht Club is like complaining about your wife to your mother-in-law.

> **SIR FRANK PACKER**, Australian who funded and led two unsuccessful challenges for the America's Cup

...and then the disastrous *Mariner* campaign, when we learned how to eat humble pie. But that in itself is something you need to learn, because in twelve-meter racing you need to have a lot of humility.

> **TED TURNER** referring to his 1974 campaign to defend the America's Cup in *Mariner*

The New York Yacht Club wants you to challenge for the America's Cup; they just won't let you win it.

> **ALAN BOND**, Australian yachtsman and Cup challenger. He won in 1983.

The America's Cup is a race of management, money, technology, teamwork, and last and incidentally, sailing.

BILL KOCH, 1996

Generally, the team that wins is not the one that is most brilliant but the one that makes the fewest mistakes.

BILL KOCH, 1996

Our day-in, day-out focus was sailing, not changing the world.

ANNA SEATON HUNTINGTON. Huntington was a member of the America[3] women's team in the 1995 America's Cup competition.

There is no greater thrill than being aboard a boat that has successfully defended the Cup.

GARY JOBSON, 1997

I've won America's Cup races by one second. That's where I come from, feet and inches, seconds. In that environment, you don't give up anything to anyone.

PAUL CAYARD, 1998

Anchoring

Our crooked anchors from the prow we cast.

VIRGIL from the *Aeneid*, Book III

It is well to moor your bark with two anchors.

PUBLILIUS SYRUS from *Sententiae*, ca. 50 BC

They anchored the high-bowed ship, moored it
Close to the shore, where the booming sea
Could not pull it loose and lead it away.

> From *Beowulf*, translated by Burton Raffel, 1963. In this 8th century Anglo-
> Saxon epic poem, the poet describes the return of Beowulf and his companions
> from Denmark to their home in the Land of the Geats.

Our sheet-anchor being obviously much too heavy for a coasting
anchor, it was at length resolved, to fix two of our largest prize anchors
into one stock, and to place between their shanks two guns, four
pounders, which was accordingly executed, and it was to serve as a
best bower.

> **RICHARD WALTER** from *A Voyage round the World by George Anson*, 1748.
> Walter is describing the method employed by Anson's flagship *Centurion* in
> replacing its best bower anchor in the western Pacific in 1742.

The bottom of the sea is strewn with anchors, some deeper and some
shallower, and alternately covered and uncovered by the sand, per-
chance with a small length of iron cable still attached—to which where
is the other end?

> **HENRY DAVID THOREAU** from *Cape Cod*, 1865

...anchors which have been lost—the sunken faith and hope of mariners, to which they trusted in vain...

> **HENRY DAVID THOREAU** from *Cape Cod*, 1865

You sail into a port where in less than a minute you must apprehend by
one panoramic glance the positions of twenty vessels, the run of the
tide, and set of the wind, and depth of the water; and this not only as
these are then existing, but, in imagination, how they will be six hours
hence, when the wind has veered, the tide has changed, and the vessels
have swung around, or will need room to move away, or new ones will
have arrived.

> **JOHN MacGREGOR** from *The Voyage Alone in the Yawl Rob Roy*, 1867

...the anchor is the emblem of hope...

> **JOHN MacGREGOR** from *The Voyage Alone in the Yawl Rob Roy*, 1867

Heh! Walk her round. Heave, ah, heave her short again!
Over, snatch her over, there, and hold her on the pawl.
Loose all sail, and brace your yards aback and full—
Ready jib to pay her and heave short all!

RUDYARD KIPLING from the poem 'Anchor Song', 1893

An anchor is a forged piece of iron, admirably adapted to its end... To its perfection its size bears witness, for there is no other appliance so small for the great work it has to do.

JOSEPH CONRAD from *The Mirror of the Sea*, 1906

From first to last the seaman's thoughts are very much concerned with his anchors. It is not so much that the anchor is a symbol of hope as that it is the heaviest object that he has to handle on board his ship at sea in the usual routine of his duties. The beginning and end of every passage are marked distinctly by work about the ship's anchors.

JOSEPH CONRAD from *The Mirror of the Sea*, 1906

There are no words that can describe the feelings of a sailor at the helm of his own ship bringing her to an anchorage of his own choice.

BILL MURNAN

And I advise all sound cruisers to anchor properly in a harbor, not tie up at a 'marina', the yachtsmen's slum.

SAMUEL ELIOT MORISON

Our anchor is our title deed to our real estate, and we can claim our property all around our coasts or in foreign countries either if we like.

FRANK COWPER

...it isn't necessary to spend every night in a marina. There is such a thing as an anchor.

KURT VONNEGUT from *Wampeters Foma & Granfalloons (Opinions)*, 1965

The single commandment of anchoring is, 'Thou shalt create scope'.

REESE PALLEY from *There Be No Dragons*, 1996

There is nothing that can ruin your cruising as much as the fear of dragging...

LIN and **LARRY PARDEY**, 1997

Art

Immediately after a storm, the air and water appear worked into a strange and fitful state—fearful to watch, but hardly to be expressed either by the pencil or the pen.

PROFESSOR ANSTED from *The Representation of Water*, 1863

The sea never has been, and I fancy never will be nor can be painted; it is only suggested by a means of more or less spiritual and intelligent conventionalism.

JOHN RUSKIN

To paint water in all its perfection is as impossible as to paint the soul.

JOHN RUSKIN

Beach

When I have seen the hungry ocean gain
Advantage on the kingdom of the shore,
And the firm soil win of the watery main,
Increasing store with loss and loss with store;
When I have seen such interchange of state,
Or state itself confounded to decay...

      WILLIAM SHAKESPEARE, Sonnet LXIV

It is a wild rank place, and there is no flattery in it.

      HENRY DAVID THOREAU from *Cape Cod*, 1865

...the grating roar
Of pebbles which the waves draw back, and fling,
At their return, up the high strand,
Begin, and cease, and then again begin,
With tremulous cadence slow, and bring
The eternal note of sadness in.

      MATTHEW ARNOLD from the poem 'Dover Beach', 1867

For water, for the deep where the high tide
Mutters to its hurt self, mutters and ebbs.
Waves wallow in their wash, go out and out,
Leave only the death-rattle of the crabs,
The beach increasing, its enormous snout
Sucking the ocean's side.

ROBERT LOWELL from the poem 'The Quaker Graveyard in Nantucket', 1946

Birds

Little birds, whiche we judged to have lost the shore, by reason of
thicke fogges which that Countrey is much subject unto, came flying
into our ships...

DIONISE SETTLE, recorder during Martin Frobisher's second voyage to
America to look for the Northwest Passage, 1577

...one of the finest sights that I have ever seen, was an albatross asleep
upon the water, during a calm, off Cape Horn, when a heavy sea was
running...we saw the fellow, all white, directly ahead of us, asleep upon
the waves, with his head under his wing; now rising on the top of a
huge billow, and then falling slowly until he was lost in the hollow
between. He was undisturbed for some time, until the noise of our
bows, gradually approaching, roused him, when, lifting his head, he
stared upon us for a moment, and then spread his wide wings and took
his flight.

RICHARD HENRY DANA from *Two Years Before the Mast*, 1840

Awkward on the land, ludicrous when struggling to rise from a smooth
sea, the albatross is most graceful and stately on the wing... Never
seeming to rest, week after week, he follows the sailing ship.

F. A. WORSLEY from *Shackleton's Boat Journey*, 1940

Boats

...the *Elizabeth* towed the pinnesse, which was so much bragged of by the owners report before we came out of England, but at Sea she was like a cart drawn with oxen. Sometimes we towed her because she could not saile for scant wind.

> **JOHN JANES,** 1587. Janes was on board the bark *Elizabeth*, John Davis captain, during Davis' third attempt to find a northwest passage from England to China.

I have a boat here. It cost me 80 [pounds] and reduced me to some difficulty on point of money.

> **PERCY BYSSHE SHELLEY** in a letter to John Gisborne, 1822

If rightly made, a boat would be a sort of amphibious animal, a creature of two elements, related by one half of its structure to some swift and shapely fish, and by the other to some strong-winged and graceful bird. The fish shows where there should be the greatest breadth of beam and depth in the hold; its fins direct where to set the oars, and the tail gives some hint for the form and position of the rudder. The bird shows how to rig and trim the sails, and what form to give to the prow that it may balance the boat and divide the air and water best.

> **HENRY DAVID THOREAU** from *A Week on the Concord and Merrimack Rivers,* 1849

The boat is like a plow drawn by a winged bull.

> **HENRY DAVID THOREAU** from *Journals,* 1858

Believe me...there is nothing—absolutely nothing—half so much worth doing as simply messing about in boats.

    KENNETH GRAHAME from *The Wind in the Willows*, 1908

The cabin of a small yacht is truly a wonderful thing; not only will it shelter you from the tempest, but in the other troubles of life which may be even more disturbing, it is a safe retreat.

    L. FRANCIS HERRESHOFF

...do not lend your boat to anyone–it never pays.

    L. FRANCIS HERRESHOFF, ca. 1950

A boat is the nearest approach to a floating, moving, safe bit of land a man can make.

    T. C. LETHBRIDGE, 1952

There isn't no call to go talking of pushing and pulling. Boats are quite tricky enough for those that sit still without looking further for the cause of trouble.

    J. R. R. TOLKIEN from *The Fellowship of the Ring*

The sweet lines of some of them all but took my breath away when I saw them for the first time in all their naked elegance. I reveled in their good looks and desired them as much for their beauty as their use.

    JOHN GARDNER

If a man must be obsessed by something, I suppose a boat is as good as anything, perhaps a bit better than most. A small sailing craft is not only beautiful, it is seductive and full of strange promise and the hint of trouble.

    E. B. WHITE from 'The Sea and the Wind That Blows', 1977

My idea of getting off in a boat is to get as far away from telephones as possible.

RODERICK STEPHENS

All right, it's true, I don't own a boat. But I have a lot of friends with boats, which anyone can tell you is a lot better.

ROBERT STONE, author of *Outerbridge Reach*, responding in 1994 to criticism that the dust jacket photo on his bestseller showed him on a borrowed boat. He later admitted that the borrowed boat wasn't even in the water.

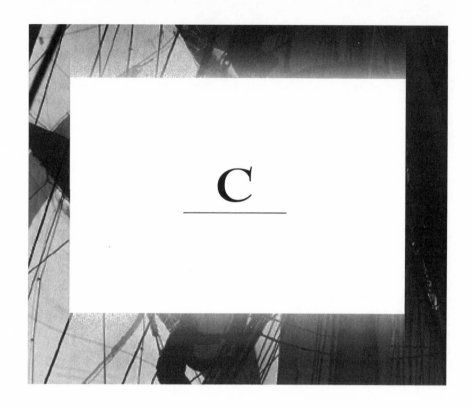

Cape Horn

The day being come the sight of sun and land was taken from us so that there followed as it were a palpable darkness by the space of 56 days without the sight of sun, moon or star as...we thus...continued without hope at the pleasure of God in the violent force of the wind's intolerable working of the wrathful seas and the grisely beholding (sometimes) of the cragged rocks and fearful height, and monstrous mountains being to us a lee shore where into we were continually drawn by the winds and carried by the mountain-like billows of the sea...

> **SIR FRANCIS DRAKE** from *The World Encompassed by Sir Francis Drake*. Drake describes conditions when his ships rounded Cape Horn in 1578.

At length being forced by the extremity of storms and the narrowness of the strait, being not able to turn to windward any longer, we got into a harbour where we rode from the 18th day of April till the 10th of May, in all which time we never had other than most furious contrary winds, and after that the month of May was come in nothing but such flights of snow and extremity of frosts, as in all the time of my life I never saw none to be compared with them. This extremity caused the weak men in my ship only to decay, for, in 7 or 8 days in this extremity there died 40 men and sickened 70; so that there was not 50 men that were able to stand upon the hatches.

> SIR THOMAS CAVENDISH describing a failed attempt to round Cape Horn, 1591

Gales were very frequent: hardly had one died down before the next came. They were so violent that many ships dragged their anchors and the men were constantly at work rescuing them. As if this were not enough, they had to endure rain, snow and hail ashore while they collected wood and water and searched for mussels or any other sustenance that could be found. Such labor was exhausting and hunger forever gnawed at them.

> Dutch sailors SIMON DE CORDES and SEBALD DE WEERT writing about a winter in the Strait of Magellan, 1598

We found such rain, hailstorms and changeable winds that course had frequently to be altered at every opportunity. In spite of it being mid-summer, the cold was appalling and frequent southwesterly gales forced us to sail under reduced canvas.

> WILLEM SCHOUTEN describing a transit of Cape Horn, ca. 1616

...from this time forward we met with nothing but disasters and accidents. Never were the passions of hope and fear so much exercised; the very elements seemed combined against us. I had to endure such fatigues from the severity of the weather, and the duty which the nature and charge of the sloop brought upon me, that really life is not worth preserving at the expense of such hardships.

> PHILIP SAUMAREZ of the sloop *Tryal*, describing the difficulties of rounding Cape Horn in 1741 during the circumnavigation by Commodore George Anson

...though Tierra del Fuego had an aspect extremely barren and desolate, yet this Island of Staten-land far surpasses it, in the wildness and horror of its appearance: It seeming to be entirely composed of inaccessible rocks, without the least mixture of earth or mold between them. These rocks terminate in a vast number of ragged points, which spire up to a prodigious height, and are all of them covered with everlasting snow; the points themselves are on every side surrounded with frightful precipices, and often overhang in a most astonishing manner; and the hills which bear them, are generally separated from each other by narrow clefts, which appear as if the country had been rent by earthquakes; for these chasms are nearly perpendicular, and extend through the substance of the main rocks, almost to their very bottoms: So that nothing can be imagined more savage and gloomy, than the whole aspect of this coast.

> **RICHARD WALTER** from *A Voyage round the World by George Anson*, 1748.
> Walter is describing the passage of Commodore Anson's squadron through the Strait of Le Maire and rounding of Cape Horn in 1741.

...I would therefore advise all ships to make their passage in December and January, if possible, so I would warn them never to attempt the seas to the southward of Cape Horn, after the month of March.

> **RICHARD WALTER** from *A Voyage round the World by George Anson*, 1748.
> Walter is warning seamen of the best, and worst, times to round Cape Horn.

...we had a continual succession of such tempestuous weather, as surprised the oldest and most experienced Mariners on board, and obliged them to confess, that what they had hitherto called storms were inconsiderable gales, compared with the violence of these winds, which raised such short, and at the same time mountainous waves, as greatly surpassed in danger all seas known in any other part of the globe. And it was not without great reason, that this unusual appearance filled us with continual terror; for had any one of these waves broke fairly over us, it must, in all probability, have sent us to the bottom.

> **RICHARD WALTER** from *A Voyage round the World by George Anson*, 1748

...these blasts generally brought with them a great quantity of snow and sleet, which cased our rigging, and froze our sails, thereby rendering them and our cordage brittle, and apt to snap upon the slightest strain, adding great difficulty and labour to the working of the ship, benumbing the limbs of our people, and making them incapable of exerting themselves with their usual activity, and even disabling many of them, by mortifying their toes and fingers.

> **RICHARD WALTER** from *A Voyage round the World by George Anson*, 1748

Indeed our sufferings, short as has been our passage, have been so great I would advise those bound into the Pacific never to attempt the passage of Cape Horn if they can get there by any other route.

CAPTAIN DAVID PORTER, U.S. Navy, aboard USS *Essex*, 1813

We had less snow and hail...but we had an abundance of what is worse to a sailor in cold weather-drenching rain. Snow is blinding, and very bad when coming upon a coast, but, for genuine discomfort, give me rain with freezing weather.

RICHARD HENRY DANA from *Two Years Before the Mast*, 1840. Dana describes conditions when his ship rounded Cape Horn.

It seemed as though the genius of the place had been roused at finding that we had nearly slipped through his fingers, and had come down upon us with tenfold fury. The sailors said that every blast, as it shook the shrouds, and whistled through the rigging, said to the old ship, 'No, you don't!—No, you don't!'

RICHARD HENRY DANA from *Two Tears Before the Mast*, 1840

We had long ago run through all of our dry clothes, and as sailors have no other way of drying them than by the sun, we had nothing to do but to put on those which were the least wet. At the end of each watch, when we came below, we took off our clothes and wrung them out; two taking hold of a pair of trowsers—one at each end, —and jackets in the same way. Stockings, mittens, and all, were wrung out also and then hung up to drain and chafe dry against the bulk-heads. Then, feeling of all our clothes, we picked out those which were the least wet, and put them on, so as to be ready for a call, and turned-in, covered ourselves up with blankets, and slept until three knocks on the scuttle and the dismal sound of 'All starbowlines ahoy! Eight bells, there below! Do you hear the news?'

RICHARD HENRY DANA from *Two Years Before the Mast*, 1840. Dana is writing of his west to east passage around Cape Horn in the ship *Alert*.

Our watches below were no more varied than the watch on deck. All washing, sewing, and reading was given up; and we did nothing but eat, sleep, and stand our watch, leading what might be called a Cape Horn life.

RICHARD HENRY DANA from *Two Years Before the Mast*, 1840

The land was the island of Staten Land, and, just to the eastward of
Cape Horn; and a more desolate-looking spot I never wish to set eyes
upon; —bare, broken, and girt with rocks and ice, with here and there,
between the rocks and broken hillocks, a little stunted vegetation of
shrubs. It was a place well suited to stand at the junction of two oceans,
beyond the reach of human cultivation, and encounter the blasts and
snows of a perpetual winter.

> **RICHARD HENRY DANA** from *Two Years Before the Mast*, 1840

Around Cape Horn in the month of May,
Around Cape Horn is a bloody long way.
Around Cape Horn with the skys'ls set,
Around Cape Horn and we're wringin' wet.

> Capstan chantey 'Hoorah for the Black Ball Line', ca. 1840

Oh, around the corner we will go,
   Round the corner, Sally
To Callao we're bound to go,
   Round the corner, Sally
Around that corner in the ice and snow
   Round the corner, Sally

> Halyard chantey 'Round the Corner, Sally', ca. 1840. The term round the corner
> refers to Cape Horn.

Round Cape Stiff we go
All through that frost and snow
Bound up for Vallypo
Then northward for Callao.

> Chantey 'Bring 'em Down'

Our boots and clothes are all in pawn.
And it's flamin' draughty round Cape Horn.
Around that Cape we all must go.
Around Cape Stiff through frost and snow.

> Halyard chantey 'Blood-Red Roses'

A hell of a Christmas Day, boys,
A hell of a Christmas Day, boys,
For we are bound for the bloody Horn
Ten thousand miles away.

Sailor's song

Familiarity with danger makes a brave man braver, but less daring.
Thus with seamen: he who goes the oftenest round Cape Horn goes the
most circumspectly.

HERMAN MELVILLE from *White-Jacket*, 1850

...in no part of the world could a rougher sea be found than at this
particular point, namely, off Cape Pillar, the grim sentinel of the Horn.

JOSHUA SLOCUM from *Sailing Alone Around the World*, 1900. He is writing
about his passage around Cape Horn in *Spray*.

I will not say that I expected all fine sailing on the course for Cape Horn
direct, but while I worked at the sails and rigging I thought only of
onward and forward. It was when I anchored in the lonely places that a
feeling of awe crept over me.

JOSHUA SLOCUM from *Sailing Alone Around the World*, 1900

Here I felt the throb of the great ocean that lay before me. I knew now
that I had put a world behind me, and that I was opening out another
world ahead.

JOSHUA SLOCUM from *Sailing Alone Around the World*, 1900. Slocum is
describing his feelings while at anchor at Port Tamar with Cape Pillar in view
during his passage around Cape Horn.

This was the greatest sea adventure of my life. God knows how my
vessel escaped.

JOSHUA SLOCUM from *Sailing Alone Around the World*, 1900. He is describing
a cold, squally night spent avoiding breakers and rocks by Fury Island,
northwest of Cape Horn.

...the westward winter passage round Cape Horn...is the wrestling of
men with the might of their Creator, in a great isolation from the world,
without the amenities and consolations of life, a lonely struggle under a

sense of overmatched littleness, for no reward that could be adequate, but for the mere winning of a longitude...

JOSEPH CONRAD from *Some Reminiscences,* later re-titled *A Personal Record,* 1912

By 10 o'clock I had lost mizzen, topsails, staysail and flying jib, so that the ship was under bare poles...it didn't stop snowing the whole morning and it was impossible to see the bows from the stern. The snow froze upon the ship very quickly, the temperature in the charthouse falling to –10 degrees C. There was no question of being able to repair the damage to the sails as no man could reach the topsail yard. During the frightful hurricane, and the day after, eleven of the crew suffered frostbite.

Captain of a French sailing ship writing of a rounding of Cape Horn in July 1900

Off Cape Horn there are but two kinds of weather, neither one of them a pleasant kind.

JOHN MASEFIELD from *A Tarpaulin Muster,* 1907

If you are in a ship in the Cape Horn calm you forge ahead, under all sail, a quarter of a mile an hour. The swell heaves you up and drops you, in long, slow, gradual movements, in a rhythm beautiful to mark. You roll, too, in a sort of horrible crescendo, half a dozen rolls and a lull. You can never tell when she will begin to roll.

JOHN MASEFIELD from *A Tarpaulin Muster,* 1907

We had bad days in the Tasman, but I never knew what the sea was till I came here.

GEORGE BLYTHE writing of the weather off Cape Horn, 1910

Westerly gale with terrible gusts. A huge wave broke over the ship at 3 AM, carrying away one of the boats and damaging two others. Standard compass torn down; binnacle damaged and compass card put out of action. Central deckhouse breached and port bulwarks pounded up to ten meters high.

Log entry from the barque *Garthsnaid* while rounding Cape Horn, January 1920

...hard by Cape Horn, that dim light of my compass on this dark
Antarctic night made me look with tenderness on these wrought
planks, flesh of the trees of my country, fashioned by human knowledge into a boat.

> Circumnavigator **VITO DUMAS** about his 1943 transit of Cape Horn

Lives there a sailor who would not rather have made a Cape Horn
passage in his own small vessel than any other voyage in the world?

> **VITO DUMAS**

I told myself for a long time that anyone who tried to round the Horn in
a small yacht must be crazy.

> **SIR FRANCIS CHICHESTER** from *Gipsy Moth Circles the World*

The Horn was the big attraction in a voyage around the world. For
years it had been in the back of my mind. It not only scared me, frightened me, but I think it would be fair to say that it terrified me. The
accounts of the storms there are, quite simply, terrifying...I hate being
frightened, but, even more, I detest being prevented by fright.

> **SIR FRANCIS CHICHESTER** from *Gipsy Moth Circles the World*

My life has narrowed to a single theme—getting through each day till I
round the Horn. The rest of the world has ceased to have any meaning.
This is my entire life and there is nothing else.

> **NAOMI JAMES** from *Alone Around the World*. She is describing her approach
> to Cape Horn on her solo circumnavigation, March 1978.

Capsize

I think I was awake when the boat began to roll over. If not, I woke
immediately she started to do so. Perhaps when the wave hit her I
woke. It was pitch dark. As she started rolling I said to myself, 'Over
she goes!' I was not frightened, but intensely alert and curious. Then a

lot of crashing and banging started, and my head and shoulders were being bombarded with crockery and cutlery and bottles. I had an oppressive feeling of the boat being on top of me. I wondered if she would roll over completely, and what the damage would be; but she came up quietly the same side that she had gone down.

> **SIR FRANCIS CHICHESTER** describing a capsize on *Gipsy Moth IV* in the Tasman Sea, January 1967

I dropped off to sleep with the wind howling a lullaby in the rigging, and the sound of water rushing past the hull coming through the planking quite clearly where I lay. The next thing I remember is being jerked awake by a combination of heavy objects falling on me and the knowledge that my world had turned on its side...

> **ROBIN KNOX-JOHNSTON** describing the capsize of his boat *Suhaili* during his circumnavigation in 1968

What was the lesser evil, I wondered: capsizing or being crushed by a wave?

> **NAOMI JAMES** from *Alone Around the World*, February 1978. She circumnavigated in *Express Crusader.*

...*Drum* rolled steadily to weather, indicating the helmsman was too low. As I cursed him under my breath we recovered, but then rolled again, and it was obviously curtains as a familiar helpless and sick feeling rose in my stomach. With the helm hard over and stalled, the whole boat shuddered and seemed to become weightless, much the same feeling I imagine in an airplane crash just before impact. Instead of a bang, we almost gently came to rest on our beam ends pinned down well and truly by a full spinnaker kissing the water and a backed mainsail held up by its preventer.

> **SKIP NOVAK** describing the capsize of *Drum* during the fourth Whitbread Round the World Race

Captains

The ships are crack sailing craft and their skippers the most experienced there are; they drive the vessels like racehorses on an unswerving course that goes straight as a die.

> Roman emperor **CALIGULA** advising a friend on the best way to get from Rome to Palestine. Translation by Lionel Cosson.

...the maister of shippes in Navigation...ought to be such a one as can well governe himselfe, for else it is not possible for him to governe his company well...

> **WILLIAM BOURNE** from *A Regiment for the Sea*, 1577

...when all hope was past of recovering the ship, and that men began to give over, and to save themselves, the Captaine was advised before to shift also for his life, by the Pinnesse at the sterne of the ship: but refusing that counsell, he would not give example with the first to leave the shippe, but used all means to exhort his people not to despaire, nor so to leave off their labour, choosing rather to die, than to incur infamie, by forsaking his charge, which then might be thought to have perished through his default, shewing as ill precedent unto his men, by leaving the ship first himselfe. With this in mind he mounted upon the highest decke, where he attended imminent death, and unavoidable.

> **CAPTAIN EDWARD HAYES** describing the death of Captain Maurice Browne when the *Delight* grounded in August 1582 off Sable Island, Nova Scotia, during Sir Humphrey Gilbert's second and final voyage to America.

...Young Gentlemen that desire command at Sea, ought well to consider the condition of his ship, victuall, and company...for there is no dallying nor excuses with stormes, gusts, overgrowne Seas, and lee-shores...

> **CAPTAIN JOHN SMITH** from *A Sea Grammar*, 1627

He should above all be an upright, God-fearing man, not allowing God's holy name to be blasphemed on his ship, lest His divine Majesty should punish him...he should not be dainty about his eating, nor about his drink, adapting himself to the localities in which he finds himself. If he is dainty or of weak constitution, being exposed to variations of climate and diet he is liable to many ailments when making the change from wholesome to coarser food, such as is eaten at sea... He should be robust and alert, with good sea-legs, inured to hardships and toil, so that whatever happens he may be able to remain on deck, and in a strong voice give everybody orders what to do. He should be the only one to speak, lest differing orders, especially in situations where there may be doubt, cause the execution of one maneuver instead of another... He should make the day his night and be awake the greater part of the night, always sleep in his clothes, so as to be promptly on hand for accidents that may happen... He must be cognizant, not ignorant, of everything that concerns the handling of the ship, everything at least that is necessary for putting to sea, and for mooring in readiness to sail, as well as all other matter needed for the safety of the ship.

SAMUEL DE CHAMPLAIN from *Treatise on Seamanship and the Duty of a Good Seaman*, 1632. Champlain describes the qualities necessary in a ship's master.

Hereafter, if you should observe an occasion to give your officers and friends a little more praise than is their due, and confess more fault than you can justly be charged with, you will only become the sooner for it, a great captain.

BENJAMIN FRANKLIN's advice to John Paul Jones, 1780

The captain, in the first place, is lord paramount. He stands no watch, comes and goes when he pleases, and is accountable to no one, and must be obeyed in everything, without a question, even from his chief officer.

RICHARD HENRY DANA from *Two Years Before the Mast*, 1840

I know who you are, but you'll have to wipe your feet.

Directions to Prince Albert of England by **RICHARD BROWN,** captain of the schooner *America*, as Prince Albert was about to go below, 1851

Often as a boy I had thought of the pleasure of being one's own master in one's own boat; but the reality far exceeded the imagination of it, and it was not a transient pleasure.

JOHN MacGREGOR from *The Voyage Alone in the Yawl Rob Roy*, 1867

Jukes was uncritically glad to have his captain at hand. It relieved him as though that man had, by simply coming on deck, taken most of the gale's weight upon his shoulders. Such is the prestige, the privilege, and the burden of command. Captain MacWhirr could expect no relief of that sort from any one on earth. Such is the loneliness of command.

> JOSEPH CONRAD from *Typhoon*, 1903

One night there came up a good beam breeze and I determined to see what the *Atlantic* could do on a reach, and when I had everything drawing well, the owner came to me and asked me to shorten sail, to which I said, 'Sir, you hired me to try and win this race and that is what I am trying to do'.

> CHARLES BARR, 1905. Barr was a legendary racing captain who successfully defended the America's Cup three times. He was speaking to the owner of the three-masted schooner *Atlantic* during a transatlantic race from the United States to England. Barr apparently did not shorten sail, and he and *Atlantic* won the race.

...I knew my skipper. He did not want to know what I thought... The man, as a matter of fact, under no circumstances, ever cared a brass farthing for what I or anybody else in his ship thought.

> JOSEPH CONRAD from *The Mirror of the Sea*, 1906

No one is lonelier than a sailing ship captain.

> ALAN VILLIERS, 1929

This is no democracy. However, I do like to hear any well thought out, reasonable suggestion. Once.

> EMIL 'BUS' MOSBACHER to the crew of the America's Cup defender *Weatherly* during the 1962 series

...a sailing ship is no democracy; you don't caucus a crew as to where you'll go any more than you inquire when they'd like to shorten sail.

> STERLING HAYDEN from *Wanderer*, 1963

A small craft in the ocean is, or should be, a benevolent dictatorship.
The skipper's brain is the vessel's brain and he must give up his soul to
her, regardless of his own feelings or inclinations.

TRISTAN JONES from *Yarns*, 1983

Circumnavigation

It is raining hard. In the salon the water is at floor level. I have made the
annoying discovery that my pump is out of order. I am soaked to the
skin. There is not a single dry place in the boat, and I cannot find a way
to prevent the rain water from leaking through many places around the
skylight and hatchways.

ALAIN GERBAULT from *The Fight of the Firecrest*. He is describing his crossing
of the Atlantic at the start of his lengthy circumnavigation, 1926.

When I left Europe to start my sail around the world, I had no generosity. I was a greedy bastard. All I could see in life was to have a boat, go
to nice places and work as little as possible. During the voyage I began
to change.

BERNARD MOITESSIER

I could not be more depressed. Everything seems wrong about this
voyage. I hate it and I am frightened.

SIR FRANCIS CHICHESTER during his circumnavigation aboard
Gipsy Moth, 1967

Maureen said, 'Well, why not sail around the world the other way?' I
had other things to think about, but her words stayed in my mind. Why
not?

CHAY BLYTH discussing his wife's suggestion which motivated him to
become the first person to sail around the world east to west non-stop. Blyth
circumnavigated in the 59-foot sloop *British Steel* in 1970–1971.

Cold

...Lest man know not
That he on dry land loveliest liveth,
List how I, care-wretched, on ice-cold sea,
Weathered the winter, wretched outcast
Deprived of my kinsmen;
Hung with hard ice-flakes, where hail-scur flew,
There I heard naught save the harsh sea
And ice-cold wave...'

> from 'The Seafarer', a 10th century Anglo-Saxon poem. Translation by Ezra Pound.

...fresh gales with hard squalls, with much snow and a large hollow sea at AM...at noon had lost sight of the Commodore and squadron, the air being so extremely thick with the large quantities of snow which fell; at the same time had it exceeding cold. Our masts and yards were all crusted over with snow.

> **PHILIP SAUMAREZ** of the sloop *Tryal*, describing conditions during the rounding of Cape Horn by Anson's squadron, March 10, 1741

The running ropes freeze in the blocks, the sails are stiff like sheets of tin, and the men cannot expose their hands long enough to the cold to do their duty aloft, so that topsails are not easily handled.

> Description of sailing off Canada in the winter 1761

Our ship was now all cased with ice, —hull, spars, and standing rigging; —and the running rigging so stiff that we could hardly bend it so as to belay it, or, still worse, take a knot with it; and the sails nearly as stiff as sheet iron.

> **RICHARD HENRY DANA** from *Two Years Before the Mast*, 1840

If you go aloft you must be careful what you touch. If you touch a wire shroud, or a chain sheet, the skin comes from your hand as though a hot iron had scarred it. If you but scratch your hand aloft, in that fierce cold, the scratch will suppurate. I broke the skin of my hand once with a jagged scrap of wire in the main-rigging. The scratch festered so that I could not move my hand for a week.

JOHN MASEFIELD from *A Tarpaulin Muster*, 1907

...for this was the coldest day of the passage. The ship and all in her appeared by the unnatural light as pale ghosts against the murk. The barometer was tumbling down, and in a word it meant snow.

CONOR O'BRIEN from *Across Three Oceans*, 1927. O'Brien circumnavigated in the ketch *Saoirse*.

Collision

A collision at sea can ruin your entire day.

Nautical adage

It is well to have on board a copy of the pilot rules and study the rules for the prevention of collision at sea. There is one very good rule not printed in the book; it is 'Might is Right'.

L. FRANCIS HERRESHOFF, ca. 1950

'Captain, have you seen any sailboats recently?'
'No.'
'Well, you should have. There's a mast and rigging hanging from your anchor.'

Apocryphal story about the captain of a merchant vessel putting into port

The rules of the road state: 'If the bearing does not appreciably change, such risk [of collision] should be deemed to exist.' Deem hell, it damned well does exist.

ROGER C. TAYLOR

We watched the distance between us close for a quarter of an hour without any noticeable change in the relative bearing of the ship. It was becoming increasingly apparent that *Swan* and a large ship were bent on occupying the same spot in the ocean at the same time...when the ship was less than a quarter of a mile away it made a panic turn to port, heeling sharply as it did. For a few horrifying seconds we were dead in her path, looking down the barrel at aligned range lights and both red and green lanterns.

> **JIM MOORE** from *By Way of the Wind*, 1991

If a proper watch is kept it is almost impossible to have a collision.

> **REESE PALLEY** from *There Be No Dragons*, 1996

Crew

If you need a crew, marry it.

> **CONOR O'BRIEN**

The only way to get a good crew is to marry one.

> **ERIC HISCOCK**

The three major factors to consider in a successful crewman are attitude, attitude, and attitude.

> **DENNIS CONNER** from *Comeback: My Race for the America's Cup*, 1987

The first thing we look for is a good attitude. The second thing we look for is a good sense of teamwork. The last thing we look for is their athletic and sailing ability.

> Maxi-racer **BILL KOCH** responding to the question, "What do you look for in a crew member?"

Cruising

Some years ago...having little or no money in my purse, I thought I
would sail about a little and see the watery part of the world.

> **HERMAN MELVILLE** from *Moby Dick*, 1851

He must have good health and good spirits, and a passion for the sea.
He must learn to rise, eat, drink, and sleep, as the water or winds
decree, and not his watch. He must have wits to regard at once the tide,
breeze, waves, chart, buoys, and lights; also the sails, Pilot-book, and
compass; and more than all, to scan the passing vessels, and to cook,
and eat, and drink in the midst of all.

> **JOHN MacGREGOR** from *The Voyage Alone in the Yawl Rob Roy*, 1867.
> MacGregor is writing of the requirements of a cruising sailor.

I was born in the breezes, and I had studied the sea as perhaps few men
have studied it, neglecting all else.

> **JOSHUA SLOCUM** from *Sailing Alone Around the World*, 1900

I'm an old man, and I should like once more to feel a deck under my
feet before it is too late.

> **JOSHUA SLOCUM** to a friend shortly before sailing from Vineyard Haven,
> Massachusetts, in November 1909. Bound for the Cayman Islands, Slocum and
> *Spray* disappeared at sea and their fate has never been determined.

In or out of 'em, it doesn't matter. Nothing seems really to matter, that's
the charm of it. Whether you get away or whether you don't; whether
you arrive at your destination or whether you reach somewhere else or
whether you never get anywhere at all, you're always busy, and you
never do anything in particular; and when you've done it there's
always something else to do, and you can do it if you like, but you'd
much better not...

> **KENNETH GRAHAME** from *The Wind in the Willows*, 1908

Surely the sailing yacht must survive, for in her alone will men find satisfaction of an instinct which drives them, regardless of progress and reason, to venture out to sea.

EVELYN GEORGE MARTIN

Our friends cannot understand why we make this voyage. They shudder, and moan, and raise their hands. No amount of explanation can make them comprehend that we are moving along the line of least resistance; that it is easier for us to go down to the sea in a small ship than to remain on dry land...

JACK LONDON from *The Cruise of the Snark*, 1911. London is explaining why he and his wife took their children and left their life in California to cross the Pacific in a small boat.

...the object of cruising is to make a complete change of surroundings, a change for the eyes, ears, and nose...a cabin should be very different from a city apartment...you should not lug along what you are trying to leave behind...

L. FRANCIS HERRESHOFF

Cruising is more than a sport. The mood of it comes over you at times, and you can neither work nor rest nor heed another call until you have a deck beneath your feet and point a bowsprit out to sea.

ARTHUR STURGIS HILDEBRAND

If there is one place in the world of Romance, it is under tropical skies in a sailing ship.

ARTHUR MASON

To my mind the greatest joy in yachting is to cruise along some lovely coast, finding one's way into all sorts of out-of-the-way coves and rivers.

R. D. GRAHAM

...when two couples are cruising together, a private head for each of them is not a luxury.

BOB PAYNE, 1988

There comes a tide in the affairs of men that, taken at the flood, sucks them swiftly away from the sea and boats and strands them for the best part of two decades on the reefs of Marriage, Career and Bringing Up Children.

JOHN VIGOR, 1990

Don't ruin a cruise by hurrying... You will ruin your own disposition and your crew's.

ROGER DUNCAN

One of the wonderful things about the cruising life is that it teaches you how little you can get along on, that to lead a fulfilling life it is not necessary to have a big pile of bucks.

STEVE DASHEW

Cruising costs as much as you have.

Nautical saying

...we were victims of the beginning cruiser's syndrome—a pervading sense that cruising meant moving.

JIM MOORE from *By Way of the Wind*, 1991. Moore is lamenting his decision, at the start of the circumnavigation which he and his wife Molly began in 1977, to leave the shelter of Coos Bay, Oregon, after only one night in port, and to sail directly into a storm.

Not only do mad dogs and Englishmen, but also cruising sailors go out in the noonday sun. To add a bit of a challenge, they lug jerry cans full of fuel down hot dusty roads; they struggle with them over slippery rocks and seawalls; they sweat like mules; they wade through the surf and clamber aboard dinghies and lay to the oars with a will on the long row to the anchorage until, at last, the tanks are topped off.

JIM MOORE from *By Way of the Wind*, 1991

Cruising sailors are poor in everything but spirit, adventure, vitality, purpose, health and desire. Sailors have made a good bargain with the world. We get to borrow it, play with it and be released from its deadening grip. We get to use it without owning it.

REESE PALLEY from *Unlikely Passages*, 1984

Cruising sailors make lists like stagnant water makes mosquitoes.

REESE PALLEY from *Unlikely Passages*, 1984

Cruising, like many things in life, is probably 25 percent planning and 75 percent execution. The lovely thing about cruising is that the planning usually turns out to be of little use.

DOM DEGNON from *Sails Full and By*, 1995

Danger

In the sea there are countless gains,
But if thou desirest safety, it will be on the shore.

> **SAADI** (Sheikh Muslih-uddin Saadi Shirazi) from 'The Gulistan of Saadi', 1258

We be three poor Mariners, newly come from the Seas,
We spend our lives in jeopardy while others live at ease.

> 16th century Elizabethan sea song

And to speake somewhat of fishes in all places of calme, especially in
the burning Zone, neere the line (for without we never saw any) there
waited on our shippe fishes as long as a man, which they call
Tuberones, they come to eat such things as from the shippe fall into the
sea, not refusing men themselves if they light upon them... The Mariners in time past have eaten of them, but since they have seene them
eate men their stomacks abhorre them. Neverthelesse, they draw them

up with great hooks, & kill of them as many as they can, thinking that they have made a great revenge.

> **THOMAS STEVENS**, 1579. Stevens sailed from Lisbon to Goa in a Portuguese ship and is describing sharks in the Indian Ocean.

Ye gentlemen of England
That live at home at ease,
Ah! little do you think upon
The dangers of the seas.

> Song by **MARTYN PARKER**, ca. 1635

Being thus arrived in a good harbor, and brought safe to land, they fell upon their knees and blessed the God of Heaven who had brought them over the vast and furious ocean, and delivered them from all the perils and miseries thereof, again to set their feet on the firm and stable earth, their proper element.

> **WILLIAM BRADFORD** from *Of Plymouth Plantation*, ca. 1650. He is describing the arrival of the Pilgrims in Massachusetts in 1620.

The sea was already roaring in a white foam about us; a dark night coming on, and no land in sight to shelter us, and our little ark in danger to be swallowed by every wave; and, what was worst of all, none of us thought ourselves prepared for another world.

> **WILLIAM DAMPIER** referring to a storm off Sumatra, 1688

We saw some of these islands of ice so high that we could observe them eight leagues off, and when the fogs cleared up, they presented us with several amusing figures, resembling fortresses, houses, ships, etc. In these unknown seas, the risks we ran were very great, for the ice is much more dangerous than the shore, as each piece of it is a floating rock against which, were we driven, there could be no hope of saving our lives. The smaller pieces of ice are even more dangerous than the larger, because they swim just level with the surface of the water, and when the sea runs high, it becomes very difficult to distinguish them.

> **JEAN-BAPTISTE BOUVET DE LOZIER** writing about his voyage in Antarctic waters, 1738–1739

...we travers'd these memorable Streights, ignorant of the dreadful calamities that were then impending, and just ready to break upon us; ignorant that the time drew near, when the squadron would be separated never to unite again, and that this day of our passage was the last cheerful day that the greatest part of us would ever live to enjoy.

> **RICHARD WALTER** from *A Voyage round the World by George Anson*, 1748. Walter is describing, with hindsight, the conditions Anson's fleet would encounter on its circumnavigation after it cleared the Strait of Le Maire at Cape Horn on March 7, 1741.

No sooner were we at sea, but by the violence of the storm, and the working of the ship, we made a great quantity of water through our hawseholes, ports and scuppers, which, added to the constant effect of our leak, rendered our pumps alone a sufficient employment for us all: But though this leakage, by being a short time neglected, would inevitably end in our destruction; yet we had other dangers then impending, which occasioned this to be regarded as a secondary consideration only. For we all imagined, that we were driving directly on the neighboring Island of Aguiguan, which was about two leagues distant...and the night was so extremely dark, that we expected to discover the Island no otherwise than striking upon it.

> **RICHARD WALTER** from *A Voyage round the World by George Anson*, 1748. In this incident the *Centurion* was blown from its anchorage at Tinian by a storm and swept toward a lee shore in the Mariana Islands in 1742.

It was Midnight, & Our Captain fast asleep. But Capt. Kennedy jumping upon Deck, & seeing the Danger, ordered the Ship to wear round, all Sails standing. An Operation dangerous to the Masts, but it carried us clear, and we escap'd Shipwreck, for we were running right upon the Rocks on which the Lighthouse was erected. This Deliverance impress'd me strongly with the Utility of Lighthouses, and made me resolve to encourage the building of more of them in America, if I should live to return there.

> **BENJAMIN FRANKLIN** from *The Autobiography of Benjamin Franklin*. He describes an incident in 1757 in which the ship carrying him to England almost ran aground on the Scilly Islands.

...the pieces which break from the large Islands are more dangerous than the Islands themselves, the latter are generally seen at a sufficient distance to give time to steer clear of them, whereas the others cannot be seen in the night or thick weather till they are under the Bows...for was a ship to fall aboard one of these large pieces of ice she would be dashed to pieces in a moment.

> **CAPTAIN JAMES COOK** on the dangers of icebergs, 1773

The risk one runs in exploring a coast, in these unknown and Icy seas, is so very great, that I can be bold to say, that no man will ever venture further than I have done and that the lands which may lie to the South will never be explored. Thick fogs, Snow storms, Intense Cold and every other thing that can render Navigation dangerous one has to encounter and these difficulties are greatly heightened by the inexpress-ible horrid aspect of the Country, a Country doomed by Nature never once to feel the warmth of the Suns rays, but to lie for ever buried in everlasting snow and ice.

> **CAPTAIN JAMES COOK** describing Antarctica, which he never actually saw, 1775

If the Bermudas let you pass,
You must beware of Hatteras.

> 19th century sailor's saying

The parting of a staysail-sheet in a williwaw, when the sea was turbu-lent and she was plunging into the storm, brought me forward to see instantly a dark cliff ahead and breakers so close under the bows that I felt surely lost, and in my thoughts cried, 'Is the hand of fate against me, after all, leading me in the end to this dark spot?' I sprang aft again, unheeding the flapping sail, and threw the wheel over, expecting, as the sloop came down into the hollow of a wave, to feel her timbers smash under me on the rock.

> **JOSHUA SLOCUM,** from *Sailing Alone Around the World*, 1900. He is describ-ing the near-loss of *Spray* in St. Nicholas Bay during his Cape Horn transit.

...man is born to trouble, to leaky ships, and to ships that burn.

> **JOSEPH CONRAD** from *Youth*, 1902

A man who is not afraid of the sea will soon be drowned, for he will be going out on a day when he shouldn't.

> **JOHN MILLINGTON SYNGE** from *The Aran Islands*, 1907

There is but a plank between a sailor and eternity.

THOMAS GIBBONS from *Boxing the Compass*

Sea room, sea room, or a change of wind.

F. A. **WORSLEY** from *Shackleton's Boat Journey*, 1940. He refers to the danger of his boat being driven ashore on the jagged, cliff-lined coast of South Georgia Island in the South Atlantic.

Darkness settled on six men driving a boat slamming at the seas and steadily bailing death overboard.

F. A. **WORSLEY** from *Shackleton's Boat Journey*, 1940. Worsley and his companions were in a 22-foot sailboat in the South Atlantic.

He who lets the sea lull him into a false sense of security is in very grave danger.

HAMMOND INNES

Mistakes made at sea are, on the surface, cause for annoyance. But to the men in charge, they're more disturbing than that; they're outrageous and inexcusable and they tell you just how vulnerable you are.

STERLING HAYDEN from *Wanderer*, 1963

The sea finds out everything you did wrong.

Singlehander **FRANCIS STOKES**

There are few dangers at sea, only problems to be solved. If you ignore the obvious solutions then you have a right to be fearful. But if you take the most basic care of yourself and your boat, you will bury your fears where they belong, deep in a thousand fathoms. Let not fear of fear keep you from the sea.

REESE PALLEY from *There Be No Dragons*, 1996

Death

True sailors die on the turn of the tide, going out with the ebb.

Sailor's saying

When life's last sun goes feebly down
And death comes to our door,
When all the world's a dream to us,
We'll go to sea no more.

Refrain from the Scottish folk poem 'We'll Go to Sea No More'

He who doesn't enter the sea will never be drowned by the sea.

Cuban/Spanish proverb

Then someone called out that all who had any gold should hang it
around their neck. Those who had, did so, both gold and anything else
of the value of gold. The women not only put on their jewelry but
handed out pieces of string to any who needed them. This is a time-
honored practice, and the reason for it is this: you must provide the
corpse of someone lost at sea with the money to pay for a funeral so
that whoever recovers it, profiting by it, won't mind giving it a little
attention.

SYNESIUS from *Epistolae*. He is describing the worst part of a storm during a
voyage in the Mediterranean from Alexandria to Cyrene in 404 AD. Translation
by Lionel Casson.

There in the harbor was a ring-prowed fighting
Ship, its timbers icy, waiting,
And there they brought the beloved body
Of their ring-giving lord, and laid him near
The mast. Next to that noble corpse
They heaped up treasures, jeweled helmets,
Hooked swords and coats of mail, armor
Carried from the ends of the earth: no ship
Had ever sailed so brightly fitted,
No king set forth more deeply mourned...

High up over his head they flew
His shining banner, then sadly let
The water pull at the ship, watched it
Slowly sliding to where neither rulers
Nor heroes nor anyone can say whose hands
Opened to take that motionless cargo.

> From *Beowulf*, translated by Burton Raffel. In the prologue to the 8th century
> Anglo-Saxon epic poem, the poet describes the sea burial of King Shild, who
> was set adrift in a treasure-laden ship.

Would it not have been far more tolerable to be carried off by any kind of
death onshore, rather than to be buried in the sea waves so far from home?

> **JERONYMO OSORIO** about the departure of Vasco de Gama and his four
> ships on the first voyage to India by way of the Cape of Good Hope,
> July 8, 1497

The waters were his winding sheet, the sea was
        made for his tomb;
Yet for his fame the ocean sea, was not sufficient
        room.

> **RICHARD BARNFIELD** from the poem 'Epitaph on Hawkins', 1595. The
> poem refers to the great English admiral Sir John Hawkins (1532-1595) who
> died at sea.

Full fathom five thy father lies;
Of his bones are coral made;
Those are pearls that were his eyes:
Nothing of him that doth fade
But doth suffer a sea-change
Into something rich and strange.
Sea-nymphs hourly ring his knell:
Hark! now I hear them—Ding-dong, bell.

> **WILLIAM SHAKESPEARE** from *The Tempest*, 1611. Ariel's Song, act I, scene II.

Toll for the brave
The brave that are no more!
All sunk beneath the wave
Fast by their native shore.

> **WILLIAM COWPER** from the poem 'Loss of the *Royal George*'. The *Royal
> George*, a ship of 100 guns, capsized and sank at Spithead, England, on August
> 29, 1782. Approximately 900 people died, including most of the crew and many
> of their families who were visiting on board.

...it is part of a sailor's life to die well.

STEPHEN DECATUR

Is this sad-colored circle an eternal cemetery? In our graveyards we scoop a pit, but this aggressive water opens mile-wide pits and chasms, and makes a mouthful of a fleet.

RALPH WALDO EMERSON from *English Traits*, 1865. Emerson sailed from Boston to Liverpool on the packet-ship *Washington Irving* in 1847.

He went out with the tide and the sunset.

Surgeon's phrase quoted by **WALT WHITMAN** to describe the peaceful death of a sailor.

I hope to see my Pilot face to face
When I have crost the bar.

ALFRED, LORD TENNYSON, from the poem 'Crossing the Bar', 1889

...that abyss of waters which will not give up its dead till the Day of Judgment.

JOSEPH CONRAD from *The Mirror of the Sea*, 1906

It ain't no place for a Christian
Below there—under sea.
For it's all blown sand and shipwrecks,
And old bones eaten bare,
And them cold fishy females
With long green weeds for hair.

JOHN MASEFIELD from the poem 'Cape Horn Gospel', 1912

Nowhere is death more painful than at sea. Ashore there are diversions; one forgets. But at sea on a windjammer there is only the little band of men. And when one goes, no one comes to take his place.

ALAN VILLIERS from *Men Ships and the Sea,* 1973. He refers to a death on the square-rigged ship *Grace Harwar* in 1929.

The sea has nothing to give but a well excavated grave.

MARIANNE MOORE from the poem 'A Grave', 1935

We weight the body, close
Its eyes and heave it seaward whence it came,
Where the heel-headed dogfish barks its nose
On Ahab's void and forehead...

ROBERT LOWELL from the poem 'The Quaker Graveyard in Nantucket', 1946

If God himself had not been on our side,
If God himself had not been on our side,
When the Atlantic rose against us, why,
Then it had swallowed us up quick.

ROBERT LOWELL from the poem 'The Quaker Graveyard in Nantucket', 1946

If an old salt lay at death's door, his family and friends watched the tide. If he survived an ebb he would improve on the flood. It was a pretty conception that the sailor's spirit would wish to float out of the harbor with the ebb and once more survey familiar scenes...before it left for another world.

SAMUEL ELIOT MORISON from *Spring Tides,* 1965

Departure

But now come, let us launch a sable ship into the boundless sea...

HOMER from *The Iliad,* ca. 700 BC. Speech of Agamemnon in Book I. Translated by T. A. Buckley.

And goodly Odysseus rejoiced as he set his sails to the breeze.

> **HOMER** from *The Odyssey*, ca. 700 BC

Then the men loosed the hawsers and took their places on the benches. Athene sent them a fair wind from the west that whistled over the deep blue waves, whereon Telemachus told them to catch hold of the ropes and hoist sail and they did as he told them. They set the mast in its socket in the cross plank, raised it, and made it fast with the forestays; then they hoisted their white sails aloft with ropes of twisted oxhide. As the sail bellied out with the wind, the ship flew through the deep blue water, and the foam hissed against her bows as she sped onward.

> **HOMER** from *The Odyssey*, ca. 700 BC

Tomorrow once again we sail the Ocean Sea.

> **HORACE** from 'Odes', 23 BC

Now, when the raging storms no longer reign,
But southern gales invite us to the main,
We launch our vessels, with a prosp'rous wind,
And leave the cities and the shores behind.

> **VIRGIL** from the *Aeneid*. Speech of Aeneas, Book III

Now was the hour that wakens fond desire
In men at sea, and melts their thoughtful heart
Who in the morn have bid sweet friends farewell,
And pilgrim newly on his road with love
Thrills, if he hear the vesper bell from far,
That seems to mourn for the expiring day.

> **DANTE ALIGHIERI** from *The Divine Comedy*. Purgatory (Canto VIII)

The wails of the women sadden'd all the coast, laments for sorrows deeper than they knew.

> Portuguese poet **LUIZ DE CAMÕES** writing of the departure of Vasco de Gama and his four ships for the first voyage to India around the Cape of Good Hope on July 8, 1497

... we wayed at Detford, and set saile all three of us, and bare downe by the Court, where we shotte off our ordinance and made the best shew we could: Her Majestie beholding the same, commended it, and bade us farewell, with shaking her hand at us out of the window.

> **CHRISTOPHER HALL,** master of the bark *Gabriel*, describing the departure in 1576 of Martin Frobisher's three vessels from Deptford, England, on the first of Frobisher's three voyages to America in search of the Northwest Passage. The queen is Elizabeth I.

Now sits the wind fair, and we will aboard.

> **WILLIAM SHAKESPEARE** from *King Henry The Fifth*, 1600. Speech of King Henry, act II, scene II.

Oh, the sun is on the harbor wall,
We must away to sea;
It's not the leavin' of Liverpool that grieves me,
But me darlin' when I think of thee.

> 18th century capstan chantey

Thus, on the 6th of May, we, for the last time, lost sight of the mountains of Mexico, persuaded that in a few weeks we should arrive at the river of Canton in China...

> **RICHARD WALTER** from *A Voyage round the World by George Anson*, 1748. *Centurion*'s passage across the Pacific actually took 14 weeks, the flagship not reaching Tinian until August 27, 1742, with the crew more dead than alive.

The ship was cheered, the harbor cleared,
Merrily did we drop
Below the kirk, below the hill,
Below the lighthouse top.

> **SAMUEL TAYLOR COLERIDGE** from the poem 'The Rime of the Ancient Mariner', 1798

Hark! the farewell gun is fired,
Women screeching, Tars blaspheming,
Tells us that our time's expired.

> **LORD BYRON** in a letter, 1809

The anchor is weighed and our rags we'll set,
Them Liverpool judies we'll never forget.

> Chantey 'Bold Riley O'

We are outward bound for the west tonight,
And the yard goes up with a cheer;
And the bells will ring in the town tonight,
And the men in the inns will hear.
And the carts will creak in the lanes tonight,
And the girls will dance to the band;
But we shall be out with the sails to fist,
And the topsail-sheets to hand.

> Author unknown

I had resolved on a voyage around the world, and as the wind on the morning of April 24, 1895, was fair, at noon I weighed anchor, set sail, and filled away from Boston, where the *Spray* had been moored snugly all winter. The twelve o'clock whistles were blowing just as the sloop shot ahead under full sail.... A thrilling pulse beat high in me. My step was light on deck in the crisp air. I felt that there could be no turning back, and that I was engaging in an adventure the meaning of which I thoroughly understood.

> **JOSHUA SLOCUM** from *Sailing Alone Around the World*, 1900

A Departure, the last professional sight of land, is always good, or at least good enough. For, even if the weather be thick, it does not matter much to a ship having all the open sea before her bows.

> **JOSEPH CONRAD** from *The Mirror of the Sea*, 1906

Anchors aweigh, my boys,
Anchors aweigh!
Farewell to college joys,
We sail at break of day.

> **ALFRED HART MILES** from the song 'Anchors Aweigh', 1907

The sound of the windlass pawls always thrills me—it's the sound of getting underway; maybe to far places, adventure, what the whole thing is about.

R. D. CULLER

...ours was no resounding departure. We tiptoed out of port like a thief.

STERLING HAYDEN from *Wanderer*, 1963. Hayden is describing the departure of his schooner *Wanderer* from San Francisco in 1959 a few tides ahead of various legal proceedings.

Even now, with a thousand little voyages notched in my belt, I still feel a memorial chill on casting off, as the gulls jeer and the empty mainsail claps.

E. B. WHITE from the essay 'The Sea and the Wind That Blows', 1977

...the narrow band of water that appears, in the first moments of departure, between the ship and the dock, designating two worlds.

JAMES SALTER from *Burning the Days*, 1997

Design

If she is right, then we are all wrong.

MARQUIS OF ANGLESEY commenting on the design of the schooner *America* in 1851

I resolved to have a thoroughly good sailing-boat—the largest that could be well managed in rough weather by one strong man, and with every bolt, cleave, sheave, and rope well-considered in relation to the questions: How will this work in a squall?—on a rock?—in the dark?—or in a rushing tide?—a crowded lock? not to say in a storm? She was to be first *safe*, next *comfortable*, and then *fast*.

JOHN MacGREGOR from *The Voyage Alone in the Yawl Rob Roy*, 1867

A sailing ship is a bundle of compromises, and the cleverest constructor is he who, out of a mass of hostile parts, succeeds in creating the most harmonious whole.

LORD DUNRAVEN

The quickest way to learn boat drawing is to draw or copy drawings, continue the practice until every point and line and their meanings are indelibly fixed in the mind. No one may expect to master the subject by simply reading it over—it requires study and practice.

CHARLES P. KUNHARDT

As a sailor judges his prospective ship by a 'blow of the eye' when he takes interest enough to look her over at all, so I judged the *Spray*, and I was not deceived.

JOSHUA SLOCUM from *Sailing Alone Around the World*, 1900. Slocum is referring to the extensive modifications he made in *Spray* while rebuilding her.

It is impossible, in this world, to achieve an ideal; and if you do not believe this, I recommend you to take a picture of your perfect ship out of your mind's eye and try to copy it exactly in metal and canvas and wood.

WESTON MARTYR

The evolution of yacht design has not been a logical and steady series of improvements.

HOWARD CHAPPELLE, 1935

...the only way that a description of this art could have been written would have been in poetry, for this method of geometric procedure is nothing more nor less than an orderly arrangement of curves and dimensions to result in a shape of complete harmony...

L. FRANCIS HERRESHOFF from *The Common Sense of Yacht Design*, ca. 1950

Any man who wants to can produce a good boat. It takes some study, some practice, and, of course, experience. The experience starts coming the minute you begin, and not one jot before.

R. D. CULLER

...sailing was the passion of my life. I can't really remember a time I didn't want to design boats.

OLIN JAMES STEPHENS

In all my years of designing, I've learned that if you have a bad boat, you are stuck with a bad boat. You can work on it and work on it, but it will never be a superboat.

JOHAN VALENTIJN, designer of four America's Cup yachts

We looked at where we got beat last time, and it was at the starting line. So the theme of the new keel isn't breakaway speed, although we seem to have that; it's maneuverability.

ALAN BOND commenting on the winged keel of *Australia II*, which won the America's Cup in 1983

What was my biggest problem in designing the keel? Why, adjustment! What adjustment, you say. Why, adjustment of the chain. What chain, you ask. Why, the chain wot holds the great white shark wot pulls the boat.

Naval architect **BEN LEXCEN**, designer of *Australia II*, the first non-U.S. yacht to win the America's Cup

Determination

They could contain themselves no longer, and began to complain of the length of the voyage. I encouraged them as best I could, trying to raise their hopes of the benefits they might gain from it. I also told them that it was useless to complain; having set out for the Indies I shall continue this voyage until, with God's grace, I reach them.

CHRISTOPHER COLUMBUS writing of his crew two days before sighting land, October 10, 1492

The sea hates a coward.

EUGENE O'NEILL from the play *Mourning Becomes Electra*, 1931

When a packet skipper got a favorable slant of wind, he carried sail until it was impossible to go aloft and take it in. There it was and there it stayed, and the gale could do with it what it willed.

ALAN VILLIERS

To be truly challenging, a voyage, like a life, must rest on a firm foundation of financial unrest. Otherwise you are doomed to a routine traverse, the kind known to yachtsmen, who play with their boats at sea—'cruising,' it is called. Voyaging belongs to seamen, and to the wanderers of the world who cannot, or will not, fit in. If you are contemplating a voyage and you have the means, abandon the venture until your fortunes change. Only then will you know what the sea is all about.

STERLING HAYDEN from *Wanderer*, 1963

Sailing the Atlantic became my compulsion. I had to go back to sea to settle the score. If you have real drive, it somehow works out.

ANN DAVISON, first woman to sail alone across the Atlantic from east to west. In 1948 her husband Frank perished when their boat *Reliance* sank during severe gales at the start of their attempted transatlantic crossing.

Difficulties

Whenever your preparations for sea are poor, the sea worms its way in and finds the problems.

Veteran singlehander **FRANCIS STOKES**

The sea's rules can be ignored only at real, physical peril, not at mere risk of social or financial penalty.

TOM WICKER from 'Rough Passage', 1988

Discovery

At two in the morning, it being very clear, we made sail again; at
daybreak we saw the land, at about five leagues distance, and steered
directly for it; but at eight o'clock, when we were close under it, the fog
obliged us again to lie to, and when it cleared away, we were much
surprised to find ourselves surrounded by some hundreds of canoes...

> **SAMUEL WALLIS** on the discovery of Tahiti in the ship *Dolphin*, 1767

We continued our course westward till the evening of Thursday the 2nd
of July when we discovered land to the northward of us. Upon approaching it the next day, it appeared like a great rock rising out of the
sea: it was not more than five miles in circumference, and seemed to be
uninhabited... I would have landed upon it, but the surf, which at this
season broke upon it with great violence, rendered it impossible... It is
so high that we saw it at the distance of more than fifteen leagues, and
it having been discovered by a young gentleman, son to Major Pitcairn
of the marines, who was unfortunately lost in the *Aurora*, we called it
Pitcairn's Island.

> **PHILIP CARTERET**'s description of the discovery of Pitcairn Island by the
> sloop *Swallow*, July 1767

Drink

...when a captain or a seaman is a drunkard it is not very safe to entrust
him with command or control, on account of the mischances that may
result while he is sleeping like a pig, or has lost all sense and discretion
and by reason of his drunkenness persists in insolence just when it is a
matter of necessity to find some way to escape from the danger. For if
he should happen to be in that condition, he will be unable to recognize
his course...and is often the cause of a vessel being lost...

> **SAMUEL DE CHAMPLAIN** from *Treatise on Seamanship and the Duty of a Good
> Seaman*, 1632

To make short this sad part of my story, we went the old way of all sailors, the punch was made, and I was made drunk with it, and in that one night's wickedness I drowned all my repentance, all my reflections upon my past conduct, and all my resolutions for my future.

DANIEL DEFOE from *Robinson Crusoe*, 1719

We are now in a great hurry for sailing and I in a sad pickle, with my whole ship's company drunk.

REAR ADMIRAL AUGUSTUS KEPPEL, Royal Navy, 1748

For grog is our starboard, our larboard,
Our mainmast, our mizzen, our log—
At sea, or ashore, or when harbour'd,
The Mariner's compass is grog.

Sailor's song, early 19th century

He seldom went up to town without coming down 'three sheets in the wind'.

RICHARD HENRY DANA from *Two Years Before the Mast*, 1840

I never knew a sailor, in my life, who would not prefer a pot of hot coffee or chocolate, in a cold night, to all the rum afloat.

RICHARD HENRY DANA from *Two Years Before the Mast*, 1840

The sailor, who only takes his one glass as it is dealt out to him, is in danger of being drunk; while the captain, who has all under his hand, and can drink as much as he chooses, and upon whose self-possession and cool judgment the lives of all depend, may be trusted with any amount, to drink at his will. Sailors will never be convinced that rum is a dangerous thing, by taking it away from them, and giving it to the officers.

RICHARD HENRY DANA from *Two Years Before the Mast*, 1840

Whiskey is the life of man,
Whiskey-o, Johnny-o!
Always was since time began,
Whiskey for me Johnny!

Whiskey is the life of man,
Whiskey! Johnny!
Whiskey in an old tin can,
Whiskey for me Johnny.
Whiskey makes me wear old clothes,
Whiskey-o, Johnny-o!
Whiskey gave me this red nose,
Whiskey for me Johnny.

> Halyard chantey 'Whiskey Johnny'

Where are my boots, me noggy noggin boots?
All gone for beer and tobacco.
The heels are kicked about and the soles are all worn out
And me toes are looking out for better weather.
So it's all for my grog, me jolly jolly grog,
All gone for beer and tobacco.
Spent all me tin on the lassies drinking gin,
And across the western ocean we must wander.

> Sailor's drinking song

Every drunken skipper trusts to Providence. But one of the ways of
Providence with drunken skippers is to run them on the rocks.

> **GEORGE BERNARD SHAW** from the play *Heartbreak House*, 1913. Speech of
> Captain Shotover, act III.

Only fools and passengers drink at sea.

> **ALAN VILLIERS**

Sea State 6. Sobriety 0.

> Radio message from a Woods Hole oceanographic team at sea back to the
> mainland

Oh Lord above send down a dove
With beak as sharp as razors,
To cut the throats of them there blokes
What sells bad beer to sailors.

> Variation of a traditional sailor's prayer as interpreted in 'Bob's Broadsides',
> *Sail* magazine

Drowning

The corpses of men float face upward, those of women face downward, as if nature wished to respect the modesty of dead women.

PLINY THE ELDER

Before he had tasted the calamity of being drowned, he knew not the safety of the boat.

SAADI (Sheikh Muslih-uddin Saadi Shirazi) from 'The Gulistan of Saadi', 1258

O Lord! methought what pain it was to drown,
What dreadful noise of waters in my ears,
What sights of ugly death within my eyes!

WILLIAM SHAKESPEARE from *King Richard the Third*, 1597. Speech of Clarence, act I, scene IV.

Now would I give a thousand furlongs of sea for an acre of barren ground; long heath, brown furze, any thing. The wills above be done! but I would fain die a dry death.

WILLIAM SHAKESPEARE from *The Tempest*, 1611. Speech of Gonzalo, act I, scene I.

...one of our ablest seamen was canted over-board; and not withstanding the prodigious agitation of the waves, we perceived that he swam very strong, and it was with the utmost concern that we found ourselves incapable of assisting him; and we were the more grieved at his unhappy fate, since we lost sight of him struggling with the waves, and conceived from the manner in which he swam, that he might continue sensible for a considerable time longer, of the horror attending his irretrievable situation.

RICHARD WALTER from *A Voyage round the World by George Anson*, 1748. Walter is describing the loss of a seaman during the squadron's rounding of Cape Horn in March 1741.

...when they got him in he was both speechless and motionless, for he had swallowed such a quantity of water that he was to all appearance dead. They held him up by the heels till he came to himself and he was perfectly well next day.

> **CAPTAIN JOHN BYRON** from *Byron's Journal of His Circumnavigations*. The incident occurred in 1765 during Byron's circumnavigation.

At length, his transient respite past,
    His comrades, who before
Had heard his voice in every blast,
    Could catch the sound no more.
For then, by toil subdued, he drank
The stifling wave, and then he sank.

> **WILLIAM COWPER** from the poem 'The Castaway', 1803

Mr. Roberts, the boatswain, whilst engaged about the rigging, fell overboard and was drowned. The life-buoy was instantly let go, and two boats lowered down; they reached the spot where we saw him sink only a few seconds too late!

> **JAMES CLARK ROSS** from *A Voyage of Discovery and Research 1839–1843*. The crewmember of the *Erebus* drowned in May 1840 during the ship's circumnavigation.

—of what use is a bottom if it is out of sight, if it is two or three miles from the surface, and you are drowned so long before you get to it, though it were made of the same stuff with your native soil?

> **HENRY DAVID THOREAU** from *Cape Cod*, 1865

The bottom of the sea is cruel.

> **HART CRANE** from the poem 'Voyages', 1926. Crane committed suicide by drowning when he leaped from a cruise ship in the Atlantic.

E–F

Equator

We just now crossed the equator. I am sure because Nancy was draining the galley sink when we crossed the line, and the water practically leapt out of the sink in its haste to reverse its draining swirl to counterclockwise.

HERB PAYSON, 1990

Fog

...through the darknesse and obscuritie of the foggie mist, we were almost run on rocks and Islands before we saw them: But God (even miraculously) provided for us, opening the fogges that we might see clearly, both where and in what danger we presently were, and also the way to escape: or els without faile we had ruinously runne upon the rocks.

THOMAS ELLIS, 1578. Ellis accompanied Martin Frobisher on his third voyage in search of a northwest passage.

...foul contagious darkness in the air.

> **WILLIAM SHAKESPEARE** from *The Second Part of King Henry the Sixth*, ca. 1592. Speech of a sea-captain, act IV, scene I.

...in the dismal fog I felt myself drifting into loneliness, an insect on a straw in the midst of the elements.

> **JOSHUA SLOCUM** from *Sailing Alone Around the World*, 1900

Fog is very terrible. It comes about you before you realize and you are suddenly blind and dumb and cold.

> **ANNE MORROW LINDBERGH** from *Hour of Gold, Hour of Lead*, 1929

The restive waters, the cold wet breath of the fog, are of a world in which man is an uneasy trespasser; he punctuates the night with the complaining groan and grunt of a foghorn, sensing the power and menace of the sea.

> **RACHEL CARSON** from *The Edge of the Sea*, 1955

Fog is...a tenuous hold on safety which a single false step can shatter, and nothing can regain: there is no cure for it except to trust and to deserve the trust of others, in continuous unbroken loyalty.

> **NICHOLAS MONSARRAT**

I loved cruising the coast of Maine. For one thing, it helped me conquer my fear of fog. Not that I have learned to feel secure in the fog, but at least I have learned how to grope without panic.

> **HERB PAYSON**, 1990

Always sail defensively in fog, and keep in mind that you may run across people who don't know what they are doing.

> **PERRY LEWIS**, 1991

Food

I had a portion cut off, which, roasted and broiled, I ate on board ship...to be able to say that I had eaten of the flesh of an animal which had never been previously eaten by any of my countrymen. The flesh, actually, is not very good, seeming tough and insipid to me.

> Portuguese captain **ALVISE DA CADAMOSTO,** writing about elephant meat he had sampled on the Gambia River in 1456

We ate only old biscuit turned to powder, all full of worms... We also ate ox hides... And of the rats...some of us could not get enough.

> **ANTONIO PIGAFETTA,** a Venetian nobleman who accompanied Magellan on his circumnavigation, 1519–1522

Item, the steward and cooke of every ship, and their associats, to give and render to the captaine and other head officers of their shippe weekely (or oftner) if it shall seem requisite, a just or plaine and perfect account of all expenses of the victuals, as wel flesh, fish, bisket, meate, or bread, as also of beere, wine, oyle, or vineger, and all other kinds of victualling under their charge...

> **SEBASTIAN CABOT**'s Ordinances of 1553

...because the weather was somewhat cold by reason of the ice, and the better to encourage our men, their allowance was increased: the captaine and the master tooke order that every messe, being five persons, should have half a pound of bread and a kan of beer every morning to breakfast.

> **JOHN JANES,** a merchant who sailed with John Davis during his first voyage to America to discover a northwest passage, 1585

Many suppose any thing is good enough to serve men at sea... A Commander at Sea should doe well to thinke the contrary, and provide for himselfe and company in like manner.

> **CAPTAIN JOHN SMITH** from *A Sea Grammar*, 1627

...to messe them foure to a messe, and then give every messe a quarter
Can of beere and a basket of bread to stay their stomacks till the Kettle
be boiled...

> **CAPTAIN JOHN SMITH** from *A Sea Grammar,* 1627

The best victual of all is biscuit, because it needs neither to be ground,
grated, salted nor diluted and it keeps for over two years.

> **GEORGES FOURNIER,** ca. 1650

Seamen love their bellies above anything else, and therefore it must
always be remembered in the management of the victualling of the
Navy that to make any abatement in the quantity or agreeableness of
the victuals is to discourage and provoke them in the tenderest point.

> **SAMUEL PEPYS,** Secretary of the Admiralty

We had not had wine for sixty days, and every man is rationed a
handful of corn a day. There are so many rats on board that we cannot
stop them from sharing it with us.

> **WILLIAM DAMPIER,** ca. 1683, writing about a Pacific crossing

...when by the storms they met with off Cape Horn, their continuance at
sea was prolonged a month or more beyond their expectation, they
were thereby reduced to such infinite distress, that rats, when they
could be caught, were sold for four dollars a-piece...

> **RICHARD WALTER** from *A Voyage round the World by George Anson,* 1748.
> Walter refers to the famine that afflicted the Spanish fleet sent to intercept
> Commodore Anson's ships on Anson's expedition against Spanish treasure
> galleons.

...at supper we ate some rats, and found them very good.

> **LOUIS ANTOINE DE BOUGAINVILLE,** French explorer in the South Pacific,
> 1768

And what d'you s'pose they had for dinner?
A parrot's tail and a monkey's liver.
Now what d'you s'pose they had for supper?
Why, black-eyed peas and a donkey's crupper.

> 19th century chantey 'Shallow Brown'

The marine people—the captain and his satellites—are bound to
provide me; and all that they have provided is yams, salt pork, biscuit,
and bad coffee. I should have been starved but for the small ham—
would that it had been a large one—which I thoughtfully purchased in
Kingston.

> **ANTHONY TROLLOPE** from *The West Indies and the Spanish Main*, 1859.
> Trollope was a passenger in a merchant brig bound for Havana.

Salt water spoils biscuits.

> **VIRGINIA WOOLF** from *Jacob's Room*, 1922

We had aboard several Somali goats. Once a month one of these was
killed, skinned, and thrown into the pot. Often we ate dried shark. I
found it dreadful.

> **ALAN VILLIERS** from *Men Ships and the Sea*, 1973. Villiers is describing the
> food on a Kuwaiti boom he sailed aboard for nine months in 1940 in the
> Persian Gulf and Indian Ocean.

G

Grounding

If you haven't run aground, you haven't really been cruising.

Bahamian sailor's adage

...wee ranne suddenly upon a rocke, where we stucke fast from 8. of the clocke at night, til 4. of the clocke in the afternoone the next day, being indeede out of all hope to escape the danger... We lighted our ship upon the rockes of 3 tunne of cloves, 8 peeces of ordinance, and certaine meal and beanes: and then the winde (as it were in a moment by the speciall grace of God) changing from the starreboord to the larboord of the ship, we hoised our sailes, and the happy gale drove our ship off the rocke into the sea againe, to the no litle comfort of all our hearts, for which we gave God such prayse and thanks, as so great a benefite required.

SIR FRANCIS DRAKE from *Drake's Circumnavigation.* The *Golden Hind* ran aground near the island of Celebes in January 1580.

...we all imagined, that we were driving directly on the neighboring Island of Aguiguan, which was about two leagues distant... We therefore immediately applied ourselves to work, endeavouring, by the utmost of our efforts, to heave up the main and fore-yards, in hopes that, if we could but be enabled to make use of our lower canvas, we might possibly weather the Island, and thereby save ourselves from this impending shipwreck. But after full three hours ineffectual labor, the jeers broke, and men being quite jaded, we were obliged, by mere debility, to desist, and quietly expect our fate, which we then conceived to be unavoidable: For we imagined ourselves, by this time, to be driven just upon the shore, and the night was so extremely dark, that we expected to discover the Island no otherwise than by striking upon it; so that the belief of our destruction, and the uncertainty of the point of time when it would take place, occasioned us to pass several hours under the most serious apprehensions, that each succeeding moment would send us to the bottom.

> **RICHARD WALTER** from *A Voyage round the World by George Anson*, 1748.
> Walter is describing the near loss of the *Centurion* by grounding in the Mariana Islands. A strong northern current carried them off the island in the dark.

A few Minutes before 11 the Ship Struck. We found that we had got upon a reef of Coral. The ship being quite fast we throw'd over board our guns, Iron and stone ballast, Casks, Hoops, staves, oyle Jars, decay'd stores & c. About 20 past 10 oclock the Ship floated, we having at this time 3 feet 8 Inches water in the hold...

> **CAPTAIN JAMES COOK**, Australia, June 1770

It is very common, amongst a certain class of men, but nevertheless an absurd and dangerous fallacy, to suppose that because a vessel is small, and of light draught, she can go anywhere without risk.

> **RICHARD T. McMULLEN**

It is difficult for a seaman to believe that his stranded ship does not feel as unhappy at the unnatural predicament of having no water under her keel as he is himself at feeling her stranded.

> **JOSEPH CONRAD** from *The Mirror of the Sea*, 1906

Out of sight of land the sailor feels safe. It is the beach that worries him.

CHARLES G. DAVIS

Only two sailors, in my experience, never ran aground. One never left port and the other was an atrocious liar.

DON BAMFORD, 1990

Gulf Stream

There is a river in the ocean. In the severest droughts it never fails, and in the mightiest floods it never overflows. Its banks and its bottoms are of cold water, while its current is of warm. The Gulf of Mexico is its fountain, and its mouth is in the Arctic Seas. It is the Gulf Stream.

MATTHEW FONTAINE MAURY from *The Physical Geography of the Sea*, 1855

In a vessel floating on the Gulf Stream, one sees nothing of the current and knows nothing but what experience tells him; but to be anchored in its depths far out of the sight of land, and to see the mighty torrent rushing past day after day, one begins to think that all the wonders of the earth combined can not equal this one river in the ocean.

JOHN PILLSBURY, ca. 1885

...the Gulf Stream and the other great ocean currents are the last wild country there is left.

ERNEST HEMINGWAY from the short story 'On the Blue Water', 1935

Landfall

The shouts of sailors double near the shores;
They stretch their canvas, and they ply their oars.

VIRGIL from the *Aeneid*, Book III

At two hours after midnight appeared the land, at a distance of 2 leagues. They handed all sails and set the treo, which is the mainsail without bonnets, and lay-to waiting for daylight Friday, when they arrived at an island of the Bahamas that was called in the Indians' tongue Guanahani.

CHRISTOPHER COLUMBUS, October 12, 1492

The first signe of land were certain fowles which they knew to be of India: the second, boughes of palms and sedges: the third, snakes swimming on the water, and a substance which they call by the name of

a coine... And these two last signes be so certaine, that the next day
after, if the winde serve, they see land, which we did to our great joy...

> **THOMAS STEVENS,** 1579. Stevens sailed from Lisbon to India in a
> Portuguese ship and describes the ship's approach to Goa.

We were in hopes of seeing land this morning, but cannot...we have run
all this day at a great rate; and now night is come on we have no
soundings. Sure the American continent is not all sunk under water
since we left.

> **BENJAMIN FRANKLIN** from *Journal of a Voyage,* October 7, 1726. After a two-
> and-a-half month Atlantic crossing on the *Berkshire,* Franklin was anxious to see
> land.

After dinner one of our mess went up aloft to look out, and presently
announced the long-wished for sound, Land! Land! In less than an hour
we could descry it from the deck, appearing like tufts of trees. I could
not discern it so soon as the rest; my eyes were dimmed with the
suffusion of two small drops of joy.

> **BENJAMIN FRANKLIN** from *Journal of a Voyage,* 1726. The ship sighted land
> on October 9, 1726, two days later than expected.

The joy which everyone on board felt at the discovery can be conceived
by those only who have experienced the danger, sickness and fatigue of
such a voyage as we had performed.

> **JOHN HAWKESWORTH** from *An Account of the Voyages...1773.* He is
> describing the arrival of Captain Samuel Wallis and *Dolphin* in the Tuamotu
> archipelago after two months at sea, June 6, 1767.

...springing aloft, I saw from half-way up the mast cocoanut-trees
standing out of the water ahead. I expected to see this; still, it thrilled
me as an electric shock might have done. I slid down the mast, trembling under the strangest sensations; and not able to resist the impulse,
I sat on deck and gave way to my emotions. To folks in a parlor on
shore this may seem weak indeed, but I am telling the story of a voyage
alone.

> **JOSHUA SLOCUM** from *Sailing Alone Around the World,* 1900. He describes his
> landfall in the Keeling Cocos Islands after 23 days at sea.

Fogs, snowstorms, gales thick with clouds and rain—those are the enemies of good landfalls.

JOSEPH CONRAD from *The Mirror of the Sea*, 1906

A landfall may be good or bad. You encompass the earth with one particular spot of it in your eye. In all the devious tracings the course of a sailing ship leaves upon the white paper of a chart she is always aiming for that one little spot—maybe a small island in the ocean, a single headland upon the long coast of a continent, a light-house on a bluff, or simply the peaked form of a mountain like an ant heap afloat upon the waters. But if you have sighted it on the expected bearing, then the landfall is good.

JOSEPH CONRAD from *The Mirror of the Sea*, 1906

It was the *Snark's* first landfall—and such a landfall! For twenty-seven days we had been on the deserted deep, and it was pretty hard to realize that there was so much life in the world. We were made dizzy by it. We could not take it all in at once. We were like awakened Rip Van Winkles, and it seemed to us we were dreaming.

JACK LONDON from *The Cruise of the Snark*, 1911. The *Snark* arrived in Hawaii after departing Oakland, California, in April 1907.

As the light grew pale, I expected the land to show, but there remained only the sea ahead, until all at once, like hands outstretched to greet the sun with spreading fingers, a row of peaks and pinnacles appeared. This was a fair landfall...

MILES SMEETON

Language

Instead of tying, Seamen alwayes say, 'Make fast!'

CAPTAIN JOHN SMITH from *A Sea Grammar*, 1627

The sea language is not soon learned, much less understood... A
boisterous sea will make a man not bred on it so sick, that it bereaves
him of his legs and stomach and courage, so much as to fight with his
meat. And in such weather, when he hears the seamen cry starboard or
port, or to bide alooff, or flat a sheet, or haul home a cluling, he thinks
he hears a barbarous speech...

> **SIR WILLIAM MONSON** from *Naval Tracts*, 1682

The language of the sea is the vernacular of a hard life.

> **GERSHOM BRADFORD**

To the landsman the language of the sailor must sound like double talk.
He knows it is English, but it does not make sense.

> **HERVEY GARRETT SMITH**

One thinks of boats in terms of a language which is foreign to those
who have never used the sea.

> **T. C. LETHBRIDGE**, 1952

...say 'sloop', 'close-reached', 'starboard', 'tiller', or 'leeward', or
murmur 'halyard', 'jibe', 'headsails', 'genoa', and the rest with an air of
familiarity ('it's a headsl', I mean), and you are instantly seen as a
dilettante, a poseur or a snob, a millionaire, and, almost surely, a
Republican.

> **ROGER ANGELL** from 'Ancient Mariner', 1993

Life at Sea

When I said I liked a sea life, I did not mean to be understood as liking
a merchant ship, with an airless cabin, and with every variety of
disagreeable odor.

> **FRANCES CALDERÓN DE LA BARCA** from *Life in Mexico*, 1843. She is
> referring to her experiences onboard the packet ship *Norman* in 1839.

At the end of each watch, when we came below, we took off our clothes and wrung them out; two taking hold of a pair of trowsers,—one at each end,—and jackets in the same way. Stockings, mittens, and all, were wrung out also, and then hung up to drain and chafe dry against the bulkheads. Then, feeling of all our clothes, we picked out those which were the least wet, and put them on, so as to be ready for a call, and turned in...

> **RICHARD HENRY DANA** from *Two Years Before the Mast*, 1840. He describes shipboard conditions during a passage around Cape Horn.

This is the pleasure of life at sea,—fine weather, day after day, without interruption,—fair wind, and plenty of it,—and homeward bound.

> **RICHARD HENRY DANA** from *Two Years Before the Mast*, 1840

I begin to comprehend that the state-room is standing on its head. Before it is possible to make any arrangement at all compatible with this novel state of things, the ship rights. Before one can say 'Thank Heaven!' she wrongs again.

> **CHARLES DICKENS** from *American Notes*, 1850. Dickens visited the United States in the 1840s.

Oh, give me again the rover's life—the joy, the thrill, the whirl! Let me feel thee again, old sea! let me leap into thy saddle once more. Let me snuff thee up, sea breeze! and whinny in thy spray.

> **HERMAN MELVILLE** from *White-Jacket*, 1850

I find the sea life an acquired taste...

> **RALPH WALDO EMERSON** from *English Traits*, 1865

I remember that some of the happiest and most valuable hours I have owed to books, passed many years ago, on shipboard.

> **RALPH WALDO EMERSON** from *English Traits*, 1865

There is nothing more enticing, disenchanting, and enslaving than the life at sea.

> **JOSEPH CONRAD** from *Lord Jim*, 1900

For sheer downright misery give me a hurricane, not too warm, the
yard of a sailing ship, a wet sail and a bout of sea-sickness.

APSLEY CHERRY-GARRARD from *The Worst Journey in the World*, 1922

There's no opium so sweet as the unguarded sunny sleep on the deck of
a boat when it's after lunch in summer and you don't know when
you're going to arrive nor what port you will land at, when you've
forgotten east and west and your name and address...

JOHN DOS PASSOS

What is there about a life afloat that has always appealed to men? It is
cold, wet and uncomfortable, often accompanied by bad food and
danger.

T. C. LETHBRIDGE, 1952

Literature

It is a strange thing, that in sea voyages, where there is nothing to be
seen but sky and sea, men should make diaries; but in land travel,
wherein so much is to be observed, for the most part they omit it.

FRANCIS BACON from the essay 'Of Travel', ca. 1625

I had already found that it was not good to be alone, and so I made
companionship with what there was around me, sometimes with the
universe and sometimes with my own insignificant self; but my books
were always my friends, let fail all else.

JOSHUA SLOCUM from *Sailing Alone Around the World*, 1900

The sea is a great university of the story-telling art.

NORMAN FREEMAN

It is not so much that sea time gives the stamp of accuracy and the quality of reality to nautical fiction, but that it directs the imagination of the writer into a field where no man dare venture without knowledge.

CAPTAIN EDWARD L. BEACH, U.S. Navy

Love of the Sea

A tender mother...is often afraid to send her son to school in a seaport town, lest the sight of ships and the conversation and adventures of the sailors should entice him to go to sea.

ADAM SMITH

As to the sea itself, love it you cannot. Why should you? I will never believe again the sea was ever loved by anyone whose life was married to it. It is the creation of Omnipotence, which is not of humankind and understandable, and so the springs of its behavior are hidden.

H. M. TOMLINSON from *The Sea and the Jungle*, 1912

Multihulls

We are surely fallen upon a new and better principle of shipping.

SIR WILLIAM PETTY describing the catamaran which he invented

It really is the most ridiculous and useless machine that the spirit of man could conceive; the doctor who invented it should return to his original profession and leave shipbuilding to those who are qualified.

SAMUEL PEPYS' diary entry in 1664 referring to the 30-ton catamaran designed by Sir William Petty

It was not a mere boat, not a mere canoe, but a sailing machine... It wasn't real. It was a dream. That canoe slid over the water like a streak of silver.

JACK LONDON from *The Cruise of the Snark*, 1911. He describes an outrigger canoe he sailed on in Raiatea, Society Islands.

In 1875...I conceived the idea of making a double-hulled sailing boat, by which great stability could be obtained with little weight and easy lines. To make the thing practical in a seaway, I devised a system of jointed connections between the hulls and intermediate structure that carried the rig, so the hulls could pitch and dive independently with but little restraint. These catamarans would sail very fast... For actual sailing, I enjoyed these craft more than any I ever owned.

NATHANAEL G. HERRESHOFF

It is my belief that a single-hulled sailing machine can not be developed that will have a higher average speed than the multihulled craft.

NATHANAEL G. HERRESHOFF

On all points of sailing, a good modern catamaran, foot for foot and sail area for sail area, is the world's fastest sailboat.

BOB BAVIER

Mutiny

The boatswain was now ordered to hoist the launch out... Particular people were now...hurried over the side; whence I concluded that with these people I was to be set adrift.

CAPTAIN WILLIAM BLIGH of HMS *Bounty*, April 28, 1789

Navigation

Who won't be ruled by the rudder must be ruled by the rock.

Nautical saying

...by her guidance the men of Sidon steer the straightest course.

ARATUS referring to Ursa Minor

A compass can go wrong, the stars never.

Tongan saying

...Odysseus spread his sail...while he sat and guided the raft skillfully by means of the rudder. He never closed his eyes, but kept them fixed on the Pleiades, on late-setting Bootes, and on the Bear...which turns round and round where it is, facing Orion, and alone never dipping into the stream of Oceanus—for Calypso had told him to keep this to his left. Days seven and ten did he sail over the sea...

> **HOMER** from *The Odyssey*, ca. 700 BC

He knows the course of the stars and can always orient himself. He knows the value of signs, both regular, accidental and abnormal, of good and bad weather. He distinguishes the regions of the ocean by the fish, by the color of the water and the nature of the bottom, by the birds, the mountains, and other indications...

> The Mu'allim, a Sanskrit document containing a description of a navigator, 434 AD

An iron needle after it has made contact with the magnet stone always turns toward the north star, which stands motionless while the rest revolve, being as it were the axis of the firmament. It is therefore a necessity for those traveling at sea.

> **JACQUES DE VITRY**, French bishop and crusader, 1218

South till the butter melts, and then due west.

> 16th century adage for sailing from Europe to the West Indies

They have one Stella Maris near the mast and a second on top of the poop. Beside them all night burns a lantern. There is a man who constantly watches the compass card and never once takes his eye off it. He gives directions to the man at the tiller, telling him how to move the bar. And this man dare not move the helm in the slightest degree except at the orders of him who watches the Stella Maris.

> **FELIX FABER** describing the use of the Stella Maris, or compass, aboard Magellan's ships during his circumnavigation, 1519–1522

Among the instruments which are necessary to Navigation is the carde for without it good Navigation cannot be made, seeing that in it the Pilot or Sayler doth see the place wherein he is, and the place whither he pretendeth to go...he seeth also what winde or windes will serve him in his course...he also seeth the distance of the way which he shall goe...

> **PEDRO DE MEDINA** discussing the utility of a chart which was called, at that time, a carde

What can be more difficulte than to guyde a shyppe engoulfed, where
only water and heaven may be seene?

> **MARTIN CORTES** from *Breve Compendio de la Arte de Navegar*, 1551.
> Translation by Richard Eden, 1561.

One of the excellentest artes that ever hath bin devised is the arte of
navigation.

> **SIR MARTIN FROBISHER**

And in keeping your dead reckoning, it is very necessary that you doe
note at the end of every foure glasses, what way the shippe hath made
(by your best proofes to be used) and howe her way hath bene through
the water, considering withall for the sagge of the sea, to leewards,
according as you shall finde it growen: and also to note the depth, and
what things worth the noting in that time, with also the winde upon
what point you finde it then, and of what force or strength it is, and
what sailes you beare.

> **WILLIAM BOROUGH**'s instructions to early mariners in the manner of
> keeping a log, 1580

No Shippe could Saile on Seas
Her course to runne aright
Nor Compasse shewe the readie waie
Were Magnes not of might.

> **ROBERT NORMAN** from *The Newe Attractive*, 1581

Thus when he all the night, with wearie toyle hath tride,
And sees the swelling seas hath set him from his waye:
Then when a little slacke of calme he hath espide,
With joyfull heart to take the height he doth assay.
His Astrolabe then he setteth for the Sunne,
Or Cross-staffe for the star called Ballastile:
And thus with help of them and declination,
How land doth beare of him, he knowes within a while.

> **ROBERT NORMAN** from *The Safeguard of Sailers*, 1584

Navigation is that excellent Art which demonstrateth by infallible conclusions, how a sufficient ship may bee conducted the shortest good way from place to place...

JOHN DAVIS from *The Seamans Secrets*, 1594

All instruments used in Navigation, of what form or shape soever they be, are described or demonstrated upon a Circle, or some portion of a circle, and therefore are of the nature of a Circle.

JOHN DAVIS, 1594

...it is not possible that any man can be a good and sufficient Pilot or skilful Seaman, but by painful and diligent practice...

JOHN DAVIS from *The Seamans Secrets*, 1594

Though it is true that the most stupid can go in their embarkations from a small island to seek a large country—since if they do not hit one part they will hit another. Yet not for this can it be admitted that they can, without art, seek small and distant islands.

Portuguese navigator **PEDRO DE QUEIROS** to the Viceroy of Peru, 1597

...when the Forestaff was most in use, there was not one Old Master of a Ship amongst Twenty, but what a Blind in one Eye by daily staring in the Sun to find his Way.

English pamphlet, ca. 1600

Among the most useful and excellent arts, navigation has always taken first place.

SAMUEL DE CHAMPLAIN

If the sea is of any other color than the ordinary one of the ocean where there is great depth, namely, dark blue, it is necessary to exercise care, and much more if at night the sea should be heard to make sounds greater than is usual.

Sailing instructions by **PEDRO DE QUEIROS**, 1606

On 1 November 1615 we passed below the sun and at midday
discovered the sun to the north of us.

> **WILLEM SCHOUTEN** from a voyage around Cape Horn

...the Sea yeelds Action to the bodie, Meditation to the Minde, the
World to the World, all parts thereof to each part, by this Art of Arts,
Navigation.

> **SAMUEL PURCHAS** from *Purchas His Pilgrimes*, 1625

It is most plain, from the confusion all these people are in, how to make
good their reckonings, even each man's with itself, and the nonsensical
arguments they would make use of to do it, and disorder they are in
about it, that it is by God's Almighty Providence and great chance, and
the wideness of the sea, that there are not a great many more misfor-
tunes and ill chances in navigation than there are.

> **SAMUEL PEPYS** about the quality of navigation during a voyage he had made
> to Tangiers, 1683

Navigation is essential; life is not.

> Hanseatic proverb

A good watch may serve to keep a recconing at Sea for some days... But
when the Longitude at sea is once lost, it cannot be found again by any
watch.

> **SIR ISAAC NEWTON** regarding the difficulties of developing a watch
> sufficiently accurate to allow the calculation of longitude, 1721

Squally. At 1 AM, providentially clearing up, discerned land right
ahead about 2 leagues making like an island with 2 homocks and by my
observation was probably an island called Cape Noir laying off the
Straits of Magellan. This was a most unexpected sight, esteeming
ourselves at that time near 200 leagues off... The Commander immediately made the signal to stand to the south West...

> **PHILIP SAUMAREZ** of the sloop *Tryal*, April 13, 1741. Saumarez refers to a
> navigational error and abrupt course change by Anson's ships during their
> circumnavigation.

When charts and pilots were unreliable and often unobtainable, when navigators had great difficulty in fixing their positions, and ships were incapable of clawing off a lee shore in many conditions of wind and sea, all seafaring was attended with innumerable perils. Only a madman or (more often) a drunkard would court danger deliberately.

N. A. M. RODGER from *The Wooden World*, 1986. Rodger is describing the dangers of going to sea in the mid-eighteenth century.

Our faithfull guide through all the vicissitudes of climates.

CAPTAIN JAMES COOK writing of the chronometer which he took with him on his second voyage, 1772–1775

The winds and waves are always on the side of the ablest navigators.

EDWARD GIBBON from *The Decline and Fall of the Roman Empire*, 1776–1787

The machine used for measuring time at sea is here named chronometer, [as] so valuable a machine deserves to be known by a name instead of a definition.

ALEXANDER DALRYMPLE in his pamphlet 'Some Notes Useful to Those Who Have Chronometers at Sea', 1779

You must be forewarned, and not therefore surprised, by the prejudices of navigators used to routine methods; their lack of knowledge will make them mistrust even the best new developments, condemning as troublesome and complex methods which they understand little about.

LE GAIGNEUR from *Pilote Instruit*, 1781

It is far better not to know where one is, and realize that one does not know, than to be certain one is in a place where one is not.

LIEUTENANT BARRAL from *Digressions sur la Navigation du Cap Horn*, 1827

...he may have to steer his way home through the dark by the north star, and he will feel himself some degrees nearer to it for having lost his way on the earth.

HENRY DAVID THOREAU

Only a sailor knows the peculiar feeling of regard and mystery with which the compass of his craft becomes invested, the companion in past or unknown future perils, his trusty guide over the wide waste of water and through the night's long blackness.

JOHN MacGREGOR from *The Voyage Alone in the Yawl Rob Roy*, 1867

The Southern Cross I saw every night abeam. The sun every morning came up astern; every evening it went down ahead. I wished for no other compass to guide me, for these were true.

JOSHUA SLOCUM from *Sailing Alone Around the World*, 1900

...even then the master of the ship, if he be wise, cries out for the lead and the lookout.

JOSHUA SLOCUM from *Sailing Alone Around the World*, 1900

Navigation *is* easy, I shall always contend that; but when a man is taking three gasolene engines and a wife around the world and is writing hard every day to keep the engines supplied with gasolene and the wife with pearls and volcanoes, he hasn't much time left in which to study navigation. Also, it is bound to be easier to study said science ashore, where latitude and longitude are unchanging, in a house whose position never alters, than it is to study navigation on a boat that is rushing along day and night toward land that one is trying to find and which he is liable to find disastrously at a moment when he least expects it.

JACK LONDON from *The Cruise of the Snark*, 1911. London was sailing a ketch with an engine from California to Hawaii.

The chronometer said that at the precise moment of taking the sun's altitude it was twenty-five minutes after eight o'clock at Greenwich. From this date it would seem a schoolboy's task to correct the Equation of Time. Unfortunately, I was not a schoolboy.

JACK LONDON from *The Cruise of the Snark*, 1911

To the layman navigation is a deep and awful mystery...The average navigator impresses the layman as a priest of some holy rite.

JACK LONDON from *The Cruise of the Snark*, 1911

Making the land, it was most important to get 'sights' for position, but the conditions for observing the sun were most unfavourable. It was misty, the boat was jumping like a flea, shipping seas fore and aft, and there was no 'limb' to the sun, so I had to observe the centre by guess-work.

F. A. WORSLEY from *Shackleton's Boat Journey*, 1940

Measured in terms of enchantment, is there anything can compare with a chartroom?

STERLING HAYDEN from *Wanderer*, 1963

Use one electronic system and you always know where you are. Use more than one and you're always in doubt.

Higgins' Law, Maine Maritime Academy

...the North Atlantic sky, after remaining clear all night, has a mean trick of clouding over before dawn when one is hoping to take star sights.

H. W. TILMAN from *Mostly Mischief*, 1966

In the old days navigators used magic to make themselves strong. But I make myself strong by thinking, just thinking.

MAU PIAILUG, 20th century Caroline Islander and navigator

If you are interested in learning celestial navigation, which isn't all that difficult, forget all of that stuff your high school teacher told you about the planet earth being an insignificant speck in the galaxy. Copernicus was wrong. The earth is, and I wouldn't steer you wrong, the absolute center of the Milky Way and probably the universe, and all heavenly bodies revolve around us. The people who wrote the Nautical Almanac know this.

Circumnavigator JIM MOORE from *By Way of the Wind*, 1991

Overboard

...we had a very terrible storme, by force whereof one of our men was blowen into the sea out of our waist, but he caught hold of the foresaile sheate, and there held till the Captain pluckt him againe into the ship.

> **CHRISTOPHER HALL,** master of the bark *Gabriel*, describing a rescue during the first of Martin Frobisher's three voyages to America in search of the Northwest Passage, 1576

Once, as they lay at hull in a terrible storm, a strong young man, called John Howland, coming on deck was thrown into the sea; but it pleased God that he caught hold of the topsail halliards which hung overboard and ran out at length; but he kept his hold, though he was several fathoms under water, till he was hauled up by the rope, and then with a boathook helped into the ship and saved.

> **WILLIAM BRADFORD** from *Of Plimoth Plantation*, 1650. The event occurred during the *Mayflower*'s crossing of the Atlantic in 1620.

One day, as one of the sail-makers mates was fishing from the end of the gib-boom, he lost hold and dropped into the sea; and the ship, which was then going at the rate of six or seven knots, went directly over him. But as we had the *Carmelo* in tow, we instantly called out to the people on board her, who threw him over several ropes, one of which he caught hold of, and twisting it round his arm, they haled him into the ship...

> **RICHARD WALTER** from *A Voyage round the World by George Anson*, 1748. Walter is describing the recovery of a seaman who fell overboard from the flagship *Centurion* in 1741.

Death is at all times solemn, but never so much so as at sea...when a man falls overboard at sea and is lost, there is a suddenness in the event and a difficulty in realizing it, which gives it an awful air of mystery.

> **RICHARD HENRY DANA** from *Two Years Before the Mast*, 1840. Dana is writing about the death of George Ballmer who fell overboard from the starboard futtock shrouds while going aloft.

...one of the boys was swept overboard by a big sea. There were no falls rove off in the lifeboats, so we couldn't lower. Many men have gone over like this, and in high wind the sailing ship can only run on.

> **ALAN VILLIERS** from *Men Ships and the Sea*, 1973. The sailor, who fell from the three-masted square rigger *Grace Harwar* in 1929, was recovered alive.

...if a person falls overboard, unobserved and untethered, on a short-handed boat in tradewind-generated sea conditions, the chance of survival is about the same as that of surviving a fall out of an airplane.

> **JIM MOORE** from *By Way of the Wind*, 1991

There's another way to lose a boat that's even more frightening than sinking—by falling off it.

> **CHRIS KULCZYCKI**, 1994

If I hadn't had the strobe light they wouldn't have seen me.

> **ALBY PRATT** on his recovery seven minutes after being washed overboard at night from *Innovation Kvarner* during the second leg of the 1997 Whitbread Round the World Race. He went overboard on December 29, 1997.

Pacific Ocean

We are about to stand into an ocean where no ship has ever sailed before. May the ocean be always as calm and benevolent as it is today. In this hope I name it the Mar Pacifico.

FERDINAND MAGELLAN, November 27, 1520

...we had completed our passage, and had arrived in the confines of the southern Ocean; and this Ocean being nominated Pacifick, from the equability of the seasons which are said to prevail there, and the facility and security with which navigation is there carried on, we doubted not but we should be speedily cheared with the moderate gales, the smooth water, and the temperate air, for which that tract of the globe has been so renowned... But here we were again disappointed; for...our sufferings rose to a much higher pitch than they had ever yet done, whether we consider the violence of the storms, the shattering of our sails and rigging, or the diminishing and weakening of our crew by deaths and sickness, and the probable prospect of our total destruction.

RICHARD WALTER from *A Voyage round the World by George Anson*, 1748. Walter is describing, in retrospect, the situation on board Anson's *Centurion* after it concluded an eight-week passage of Cape Horn and finally entered the Pacific Ocean in May 1741.

There is, one knows not what sweet mystery about this sea, whose gently awful stirrings seem to speak of some hidden soul beneath; like those fabled undulations of the Ephesian sod over the buried Evangelist St John. And meet it is, that over these sea-pastures, wide-rolling prairies and Potters' Fields of all four continents, the waves should rise and fall, and ebb and flow unceasingly; for here, millions of mixed shades and shadows, drowned dreams, somnambulisms, reveries; all that we call lives and souls, lie dreaming, dreaming, still; tossing like slumberers in their beds; the ever-rolling waves but made so by their restlessness.

HERMAN MELVILLE from *Moby Dick*, 1851

...this mysterious, divine Pacific zones the world's whole bulk about; makes all coasts one bay to it; seems the tide-beating heart of earth.

HERMAN MELVILLE from *Moby Dick*, 1851

To cross the Pacific Ocean, even under the most favorable circumstances, brings you for many days close to nature, and you realize the vastness of the sea.

JOSHUA SLOCUM from *Sailing Alone Around the World*, 1900

...we found ourselves in the midst of one of the loneliest of the Pacific solitudes. In the sixty days we were crossing it we sighted no sail, lifted no steamer's smoke above the horizon. A disabled vessel could drift in this deserted expanse for a dozen generations, and there would be no rescue.

JACK LONDON from *The Cruise of the Snark*, 1911. London is referring to a passage from Hawaii to Tahiti in 1907.

Passages

There are many advantages in sea-voyaging, but security is not one of them.

> **SAADI** (Sheikh Muslih-uddin Saadi Shirazi) from 'The Gulistan of Saadi', 1258

Gentyl maryners on a bonne viage
Hoyce up the sayle and let God stere;
In ye bonaventur makyng your passage
It is ful sea the wether fayre and clere.

> **PIERRE GARCIE** from *Routier (The Rutter of the Sea)*, 1520

...all which time we had no night, but that easily, and without any impediment we had when we were so disposed, the fruition of our bookes, and other pleasures to passe away the time: a thing of no small moment, to such as wander in unknowen seas, and long navigations, especially, when both the winds and raging surges do passe their common and wonted course.

> **DIONISE SETTLE** writing about six weeks of good weather in the high latitudes during Martin Frobisher's second voyage to America to look for the Northwest Passage, 1577

There is really something strangely cheering to the spirits in the meeting of a ship at sea, containing a society of creatures of the same species and in the same circumstances with ourselves, after we had been long from the separated and excommunicated as it were from the rest of mankind.

> **BENJAMIN FRANKLIN** writing about a two-and-a-half month Atlantic crossing on the *Berkshire*, September 23, 1726

...our passage would prove at least three times as long as we first expected; and consequently we had the melancholy prospect, either of dying by the scurvy, or perishing with the ship for want of hands to navigate her.

> **RICHARD WALTER** from *A Voyage round the World by George Anson*, 1748. Walter is describing conditions on Anson's *Centurion* in 1742, when crossing the Pacific from Mexico to the Mariana Islands took 14 weeks instead of 3.

'Sail ho!' Neither land nor sail had we seen since leaving San Diego; and anyone who has traversed the length of a whole ocean alone, can imagine what an excitement such an announcement has produced on board.

> **RICHARD HENRY DANA** from *Two Years Before the Mast*, 1840. The sail, encountered while the ship was rounding Cape Horn, turned out to be an iceberg.

I lashed the helm and my vessel held her course, and while she sailed I slept.

> **JOSHUA SLOCUM** from *Sailing Alone Around the World*, 1900

No one can know the pleasure of sailing free over the great oceans save those who have had the experience.

> **JOSHUA SLOCUM** from *Sailing Alone Around the World*, 1900

The world faded as the procession of the weeks marched by. The world faded until at last there ceased to be any world except the little world of the *Snark*, freighted with her seven souls and floating on the expanse of the waters. Our memories of the world, the great world, became like dreams of former lives we had lived somewhere before we came to be born on the *Snark*.

> **JACK LONDON** from *The Cruise of the Snark*, 1911. London is describing a 60-day passage from Hawaii to Tahiti in 1907.

Does one actually enjoy these long passages? Rather a difficult question to answer. I would not undertake a long passage for its sake alone, but as the only possible means of reaching a new and desirable cruising ground they are well worth while.

> **R. D. GRAHAM**

Only the flicker of two or three fires astern betrayed the presence of a tiny lonesome world lost in a lonely ocean.

> **WILLIAM A. ROBINSON**

...he has returned to his mother sea only on her own terms. He cannot control or change the ocean as, in his brief tenancy of earth, he has subdued and plundered the continents. In the artificial world of his cities and towns, he often forgets the true nature of his planet and the long vistas of its history, in which the existence of the race of men has occupied a mere moment of time. The sense of all these things comes to him most clearly in the course of a long ocean voyage, when he watches day after day the receding rim of the horizon, ridged and furrowed by waves; when at night he becomes aware of the earth's rotation as the stars pass overhead; or when, alone on this world of water and sky, he feels the loneliness of his earth in space.

RACHEL CARSON from *The Sea Around Us*, 1951

The ship runs free. Oh the magic of those words! Free as a cloud she goes, with the sun in the east a brass balloon and the shadows adrift in her lee, undulating shadows that swell and collapse in convoluted patterns.

STERLING HAYDEN from *Wanderer*, 1963

Long voyages—any voyages—in a small sailing craft are most complex operations when they are carried out properly, in a seamanlike manner. The idea of escaping the problems of life by sailing away is a fable.

TRISTAN JONES from *Yarns*, 1983

...once the view is landless, there's no foretelling what any passage may bring.

RICHARD MORRIS DEY from 'The Loss of the Schooner Kestrel', 1988

Ocean sailing does not cease at sunset, or when a motel is reached, or when one is tired of it. It goes on and on, day and night, hour after hour, seasickness and discomfort notwithstanding, hammering seas be damned.

TOM WICKER from 'Rough Passage', 1988

...picking weather in which to cross is a lot like picking through a junkyard looking for engine parts—nothing is ideal, but if you're patient, something you can use will turn up.

HERB PAYSON, 1989

A tradewind starts gently, without gusts—a huge ocean of air that slowly and resolutely begins to move with ever-increasing strength. Suddenly everything comes to life. Spirits rise as the sails fill. The boat heels slightly and moves ahead. The almost oppressive silence gives way to the sound of the bow cutting through the water. Gone is the sea's glassy surface, and with it the terrible glare. Close the hatches and ports! We're sailing again!

JIM MOORE from *By Way of the Wind*, 1991

Phenomena

During these tempests the body of St. Elmo appeared to us several times. In particular on a night when the sky was especially dark and the storm especially violent, the saint appeared in the guise of a lighted torch at the head of the mainmast; here he remained for more than two hours, a great comfort to us all, for before his arrival we were in despair, expecting death any moment to overtake us. When this holy light was about to leave us, it became so bright to our eyes that we were like blind men calling for mercy... Suddenly the fire vanished and the sea grew calm, and a great multitude of birds settled upon the ship.

ANTONIO PIGAFETTA describing St. Elmo's fire during Magellan's circumnavigation, 1519–1522

This morning, one of our companie looking over boord saw a mermaid, and calling up some of the companie to see her, one more came up, and by that time shee was come close to the ship's side, looking earnestly on the men: a little after, a sea came and overturned her: from the navill upward, her backe and breasts were like a woman's...her body as big as one of us; her skin very white; and long haire hanging downe behinde, of colour black: in her going down they saw her tayle, which was like the tayle of a porposse, and speckled like a macrell.

From the log of **HENRY HUDSON**, while sailing in the Barents Sea on June 15, 1608

The object was discovered to be an enormous serpent, with head and shoulders kept about four feet constantly above the surface of the sea, and as nearly as we could approximate by comparing it with the length of what our main-topsail yard would show in the water, there was at the very least 60 feet of the animal [visible], no portion of which was, to our perception, used in propelling it through the water... The diameter of the serpent was about 15 or 16 inches behind the head, which was, without any doubt, that of a snake, and it was never, during the 20 minutes that it continued in sight of our glasses, once below the surface of the water; its colour a dark brown, with yellowish white about the throat. It had no fins, but something like the mane of a horse, or rather a bunch of seaweed, washed about its back.

> **PETER M'QUAHE**, captain of the frigate HMS *Daedalus*, writing about a sea serpent observed by his officers and crew in the South Atlantic in August 1848

Pirates

Fifteen men on a dead man's chest
Yo ho ho and a bottle of rum.
Drink and the devil have done for the rest,
Yo ho ho and a bottle of rum.

> Traditional sailor's song

Ports and Places

Let us run into a safe harbor.

> **ALCAEUS**, ca. 600 BC

I take this to be one of the most unhealthy places in the world, at least at this season. The airs are extremely violent and the sun so scorching that it is difficult breathing.

> **CAPTAIN JOHN BYRON** from *Byron's Journal of His Circumnavigations*. He is describing Tinian which he reached with *Dolphin* and *Tamar* in July 1765.

Surely, surely, slumber is more sweet than toil, the shore
Than labour in the deep mid-ocean, wind and wave and oar;
O rest ye, brother mariners, we will not wander more.

ALFRED, LORD TENNYSON, from the poem 'The Lotos-Eaters', 1832

...Provincetown is directly in the way of the navigator, and he is lucky
who does not run afoul of it in the dark. It is situated on one of the
highways of commerce, and men from all parts of the globe touch there
in the course of a year.

HENRY DAVID THOREAU from *Cape Cod*, 1865

A harbor, even if it is a little harbor, is a good thing.

SARAH ORNE JEWETT from 'River Driftwood', 1881

Islanders are always the kindest people in the world, and I met none
anywhere kinder than the good hearts of this place.

JOSHUA SLOCUM from *Sailing Alone Around the World*, 1900, writing about
the Azores

Ports are no good—ships rot, men go to the devil.

JOSEPH CONRAD from *The Mirror of the Sea*, 1906

Ports are necessities, like postage stamps or soap, but they seldom seem
to care what impressions they make.

ELIZABETH BISHOP from 'Arrival at Santos' in *Questions of Travel*, 1965

...Key West, an island made quirky by a dangerous slant of light angling
from the tropics.

THOMAS SANCHEZ from *Mile Zero*, 1989

...St Lucia, a high and implausibly green island that invites you to drop
just about everything—career included—and stay awhile...

GEOFFREY NORMAN, 1990

Prayer

But the Lord hurled a great wind upon the sea, and there was a mighty tempest on the sea, so that the ship threatened to break up. Then the mariners were afraid, and each cried to his god; and they threw the wares that were in the ship into the sea, to lighten it for them. But Jonah had gone down into the inner part of the ship and had lain down, and was fast asleep. So the captain came and said to him, 'What do you mean, you sleeper? Arise, call upon your god! Perhaps the god will give a thought to us, that we do not perish'.

> The Holy Bible, Revised Standard Version, Jonah 1:4-6. Jonah was en route from Joppa to Tarshish when the storm arose. The sailors subsequently threw him into the sea and he was swallowed by a great fish.

Ye gods, presiding over lands and seas,
And you who raging winds and waves appease,
Breathe on our swelling sails a prosp'rous wind,
And smooth our passage to the port assign'd.

> **VIRGIL** from the *Aeneid*. Prayer of Anchises, father of Aeneas, Book III

Item, that morning and evening prayer, with other common services appointed by the kings Majestie, and lawes of this Realme to be read and saide in every ship daily by the minister...and the Bible or paraphrases to be read devoutly and Christianly to Gods honour, and for his grace to be obtained, and had by humble and heartie praier of the navigants accordingly.

> **SEBASTIAN CABOT**'s Ordinances of 1553

Oh Lord, have mercy,
Thy sea is so large
And my ship is so small.

> Breton fisherman's prayer

O most powerful and glorious Lord God, at whose command the winds blow, and lift up the waves of the sea, and who stillest the rage thereof; We thy creatures, but miserable sinners, do in this our great distress cry unto thee for help; Save, Lord, or else we perish.

> Book of Common Prayer, 1662

Racing

When you keep getting headed, it's time to tack.

> Racer's adage

Races are won at night.

> Racer's adage

I had sailed this morning with His Majesty in one of the yachts or pleasure boats, being very excellent sailing vessels. It was on a wager between his other new pleasure boat, built frigate-like, and one of the Duke of York's; the wager one hundred pounds sterling, the race from Greenwich to Gravesend and back. The King lost in the going, the wind being contrary, but saved stakes in returning.

> **JOHN EVELYN**'s diary entry for October 1, 1661, recording the first known yacht race

The Gentlemen, about 18 or 20 in number, who sail for the prize have come to a resolution to be dressed in aquatic uniforms.

> London newspaper commenting on the origin of team uniforms for racing, 1775

What we want is a plain and simple rule 'with no plus' in it; who knows what 'plus' is? I don't know what 'plus' is. You take the length on deck and add it to the length on the waterline and divide by two, and you have a plain and simple rule 'with no plus in it'.

> ALANSON J. PRIME discussing racing yacht measurements at the founding convention of the New York Yacht Racing Association, 1889

The point has been raised that it may be against the spirit of ocean racing to 'build to the rule', or, in other words, to build a vessel in which every advantage is taken of gaining speed that the rule allows. I believe that it is a short-sighted policy not to build to the rule, for the result of building to it will be to produce a type of ocean racing yacht which will be extremely fast without any sacrifice of seagoing ability.

> EVELYN GEORGE MARTIN, 1928

Drill, practice and drill, and practice again. Sail for as long as possible every day until you long for an excuse for a lay day.

> J-boat skipper in the 1930s describing the routine of getting ready to race the enormous craft

One of the ambitions of every deep sea yachtsman is to participate in the Fastnet Race. It gives him prestige so that to some degree he can look down with a feeling of superiority on yachtsmen who haven't had the opportunity.

> IRVING JOHNSON, 1933

I have learned for the first time that the fastest yacht does not win the race.

> CHARLES NICHOLSON, designer of the J-boat *Endeavour*, after the British yacht lost the 1934 America's Cup series to Harold Vanderbilt's slower but better handled *Rainbow*

The wood ain't growing yet that'll beat *Bluenose*.

ANGUS WALTERS

It will be too bad if yachts are spoiled so they are no longer good for pleasure sailing or relaxed comfort.

L. FRANCIS HERRESHOFF lamenting rule changes that made racing yachts faster but less habitable, ca. 1950

I'm not particularly interested in racing or record passages. After all, I go to sea to get away from the competitive rat-race, not to join it.

JIM WHARRAM, designer of Britain's first trans-ocean cruising catamaran

The ultimate basis of success in racing is the skipper's decisive command of himself, his boat, and the situation.

STUART H. WALKER

Winning a 12-meter race is really a function of how many mistakes you make, not how brilliant you are. You don't win on brilliance; you lose on mistakes.

GARY JOBSON

When you're behind, you keep trying to tack to get away, for hours and hours, and it's so hard to do that it feels like somebody has taken a whip and beaten you on the back.

TED TURNER describing practicing for the America's Cup

The chance for mistakes is about equal to the number of crew squared...

TED TURNER

There are only so many moves and so many countermoves. There's not much to it, actually. The problem is the variables.

GARY JOBSON on match racing

Sailboat racing is not a matter of life and death—it's much more serious than that.

Bumper sticker

A boat's position at the start is the single greatest determining factor in the average yacht race.

BOB BAVIER

Make up your mind to get over a few seconds earlier than you think you should. A poor starter is almost always late. It is the good ones that occasionally slip up and get over too early.

BOB BAVIER

...more races are won and lost on the windward than any other leg.

BOB BAVIER

Racing without a knowledge of the current is like walking up an escalator that is going down.

BOB BAVIER

It's like standing under a cold shower tearing up five-pound notes.

English yachtsman **EDWARD HEATH** describing the thrills of sailboat racing

If you're winning, don't change what you're doing.

Yacht racing adage

Where else in the sporting world would the press proclaim as 'Grand Prix Racing' the sorry spectacle of twelve men slumped over a wet rail, slogging along at eight knots on a $200,000 object that is obsolete the next season?

GARRY HOYT

The secret of winning is very simple: do everything reasonably well and make no mistakes.

Maxi-racer **BILL KOCH**

No, it isn't. There's one rich man on board and there's twenty-five poor men and they enjoy it more than the rich man does.

JIM KILROY's response when asked if maxi-yacht racing is a rich man's sport

My preference has always been for long-distance racing, ocean racing, not around the buoys...it shows how good your crew and your boat are in all kinds of conditions over a long period of time.

HUEY LONG, maxi-yacht racer and owner of a series of yachts named *Ondine*

The crew is the key part of winning a race.

JIM KILROY, maxi-yacht racer

I don't rant at my crew, but in events like the Whitbread Round the World Race, you cannot practice democracy.

PIERRE FEHLMAN, Swiss yachtsman and maxi-boat owner and racer

At some point during the race you might be wet, cold, scared, uncomfortable, or even bleeding. This is normal. This is part of the fun.

JANICE MOHLHENRICH, 1997

...it's blowing hard. With black snow squalls coming in from behind. And the yacht is on the verge of being out of control. The spray coming over the windward deck is turning to ice particles. The decks are covered in ice. The coils of rope in the bottom of the cockpits are full of snow. And it's so bitterly cold.

PETER BLAKE on board *Ocean Conquest* describing the second leg (South Africa to Australia) of the 1997 Whitbread Round the World Race

We have been close reaching now for 20 hours in 25-30 knots of wind. That produces a three-alarm fire. At this stage of the race, it is not very fun. We are all very tired and wet and the non-stop pounding of the water on your face and body drains everything out of you. Just trying to support yourself below in the nav station or getting dressed and undressed is a major workout when the boat is jolting along like this.

Our boat is leaking badly from the deck and mast area. This has made the interior extra damp on this trip. With no heater and no bilge pump, everything is damp, the sleeping bags, our clothes, the charts, the toilet paper, everything. We are looking forward to touching something dry.

> **PAUL CAYARD**, skipper of *EF Language*, November 24, 1997, during the second leg of the Whitbread Round the World Race

It's the fastest boat, and the fastest crew that will win, but you've got to finish to win.

> **ROSS FIELD**, New Zealand yachtsman and skipper of *Yamaha*, the winner in the 1993–1994 Whitbread 60 competition, discussing the 1997–1998 Whitbread Round the World Race

Yacht racing is not listed as a safe activity in life.

> **CHRIS DICKSON**, while preparing for the 1997–1998 Whitbread Round the World Race

Anyone in their right mind is afraid of the next leg.

> **PAUL CAYARD**, skipper of *EF Language* on January 22, 1998, before the start of the fifth leg (Auckland to São Sebastião, Brazil) in the 1997–1998 Whitbread Round the World Race. Cayard is replying to the question: Is anyone on board afraid of the next leg around Cape Horn, or is it the more wind, the better?

Everything's broken, everybody's hurt, we stink, the boat stinks, we haven't been out of our foul-weather gear for 16 days.

> **KIMO WORTHINGTON** describing conditions on *EF Language* on Leg 2 of the 1997–1998 Whitbread Around the World Race, 1998

Religion

What fear of the waves of the sea has he whose pilot is Noah?

> **SAADI** (Sheikh Muslih-uddin Saadi Shirazi) from 'The Gulistan of Saadi', 1258

We are as near to heaven by sea as by land.

> **SIR HUMPHREY GILBERT**, 1583. His frigate *Squirrel* sank in an Atlantic storm shortly after he said this, he and all the crew perishing.

He that will learn to pray, let him go to sea.

> **GEORGE HERBERT** from *Jacula Prudentum*, 1651

I had long before this repented me of that roving course of life, but never with such concern as now. I did also call to mind the many miraculous acts of God's providence towards me in the whole course of my life, of which kind few men have met with the like. For all these I returned thanks in a peculiar manner, and thus once more desired God's assistance, and composed my mind as well as I could in the hopes of it, and as the events showed, I was not disappointed in my hopes.

> **WILLIAM DAMPIER** from *A New Voyage Around the World*. Dampier is describing his thoughts while in an outrigger canoe during a storm off Sumatra in May 1688.

Eternal Father, Strong to save,
Whose arm hath bound the restless wave,
Who bidd'st the mighty ocean deep
Its own appointed limits keep:
O, hear us when we cry to thee
For those in peril on the sea!

> 'The Navy Hymn' by **WILLIAM WHITING**, 1860

If you spend the night alone in an open boat in a thunderstorm, it will bring you closer to God than going to church forty Sundays.

> **L. FRANCIS HERRESHOFF**

I believe in the Bible because it don't mention no sea in Paradise.

JOHN FOWLES from *Shipwreck*, 1974. He quotes the remark of an old sailor to Lord Fisher.

In the great days of sail, before man's inventions and gadgets had given him false confidence in his power to conquer the ocean, seamen were the most religious of all workers on land or sea.

SAMUEL ELIOT MORISON

Rigging

Behold, at last,
Each tall and tapering mast
Is swung into its place;
Shrouds and stays
Holding it firm and fast!

HENRY WADSWORTH LONGFELLOW from the poem 'The Building of the Ship', 1849

Just as I was thinking about taking in the sail the jibstay broke at the masthead, and fell, jib and all, into the sea.

JOSHUA SLOCUM from *Sailing Alone Around the World*, 1900

Upon acquiring his first boat the yachtsman discovers that its use is going to involve intimate personal contact with rope and cordage, and to a far greater extent than he ever anticipated.

HERVEY GARRETT SMITH from *The Arts of a Sailor*

Life is too short to splice wire rope.

BERNARD MOITESSIER

Frenchman and I were sent aloft to make fast the fore upper topgallant sail this morning, in a hard squall. We climbed into the shrouds at 6 AM in pitch darkness. It was raining steadily and big seas were coming aboard. The wind had a cold sting in it which gradually froze us to the marrow.

We were up there for nearly two hours, while a cold and cheerless dawn broke over the wind-torn sea, and we fought with the sodden sails until the work became a pain and a purgatory. The rain persistently drove at us, making our caps sodden and our oilskins sodden; the cold water trickled down through crevices which nothing but water could find. Our fingers were stiff and blue with cold and red from tears on jagged wire gear...

RONALD WALKER from *Men Ships and the Sea* by Alan Villiers, 1973. Walker and Villiers shipped aboard the three-masted square rigger *Grace Harwar* to make a film about sailing ships. This diary entry describes conditions off the coast of New Zealand in May 1929. Walker died shortly thereafter in an accident aloft. He had been at sea only two months; his death added to the *Grace Harwar*'s reputation as a mankiller.

Sailing

...when the sun had set, and darkness came on, then they slept near the hawsers of their ships. But when the mother of dawn, rosy-fingered morning, appeared, straightway then they set sail...and to them far-darting Apollo sent a favorable gale. They erected the mast and expanded the white sails. The wind streamed into the bosom of the sail; and as the vessel briskly ran, the dark wave roared loudly around the keel.

HOMER from *The Iliad*, ca. 700 BC

And when they had taken up the anchors, they committed themselves unto the sea...and hoisted up the mainsail to the wind...

The Holy Bible, King James Version, Acts 27:40

I did not wish to take a cabin passage, but rather to go before the mast and on the deck of the world, for there I could best see the moonlight amid the mountains. I do not wish to go below now.

HENRY DAVID THOREAU from *Walden*, 1854

Thus we sailed, not being able to fly, but as next best, making a long furrow...

HENRY DAVID THOREAU

...we bounded merrily over before a smacking breeze, with a devil-may-care look in our faces, and our boat a white bone in its mouth...

HENRY DAVID THOREAU

To go to sea! Why, it is to have the experience of Noah—to realize the deluge. Every vessel is an ark.

HENRY DAVID THOREAU from *Cape Cod*, 1865

The day was perfect, the sunlight clear and strong. Every particle of water thrown into the air became a gem, and the *Spray*, making good her name as she dashed ahead, snatched necklace after necklace from the sea...

JOSHUA SLOCUM, from *Sailing Alone Around the World*, 1900. He is writing about *Spray*'s departure from Boston on the first day of his voyage around the world.

Sailing became a compulsion: there lay the boat, swinging to her mooring, there blew the wind; I had no choice but to go.

E. B. WHITE from 'The Sea and the Wind that Blows', 1977

I cannot not sail.

E. B. WHITE from 'The Sea and the Wind that Blows', 1977

I enjoyed every boat I ever sailed. It doesn't really matter what size boat you're sailing. The sport is the same, whether it's a Penguin or an Interclub dinghy or a Laser or a twelve-meter or a Class A offshore racer.

TED TURNER, 1979

I've spent a lot of time sailing, but I've spent a lot more time working, and had I not been successful in business, I could never have achieved success in sailing. It took money, and that came from my business. Your career provides for your sailing, so your career should come first.

TED TURNER

You can be sure spring is nigh when one kind of sap is rising in the sugar bush and another kind shows up down at the local boatyard with an ice pick.

FRED BROOKS

A fresh to strong easterly sang in the rigging and we hoisted the mizzen staysail, whizzing along until, in an extra-strong gust, it parted at the tack with a crack they must have heard all the way to Philadelphia. But *Sundowner* and we laughed as we handed the staysail, for on this, the second day out, we had our sea legs, whilst she had her crew and she knew it.

TRISTAN JONES from *Yarns*, 1983

I'd rather be sailing.

Bumper sticker

Sailing is a good sport. You don't have to beat up the other guy, like you do in boxing or football; you just try to outsmart him, and outsail him, and then you go out and have a beer with him.

JOHN KOLIUS

What the landsman senses and perhaps envies is exactly what grabs me at odd moments in a small boat in August. Here—for the length of this puff, this lift and heel—I am almost in touch with the motions of my planet: not at one with them but riding a little crest and enjoying the view.

ROGER ANGELL from 'Ancient Mariner', 1993

It is hard to become a true sailor if you get into the habit of using a motor.

Circumnavigator **JACQUES-YVES LE TOUMELIN**

There is a compelling simplicity about making headway under sail: no moving parts, no lubrication or fuel, no noise—just the wind in the sails and the boat in harmony with nature.

JOHN BEATTIE from *The Breath of Angels*, 1997

Sailing is the second sexiest sport.

DR. RUTH WESTHEIMER, 1998

Sailors

They that go down to the sea in ships, that do business in great waters; These see the works of the Lord, and his wonders in the deep.

The Holy Bible, King James Version, Psalms 107:23-24

...the Athenians with their long experience in naval matters pay their own men only three obols, not because of lack of funds but to keep the men from being corrupted by having too much; otherwise some would harm their bodies by squandering money on the sort of things that injure the health and others, with no pay owing to them to serve as a sort of hostage, would jump ship.

Athenian admiral discussing sailors and their pay, as reported by **THUCYDIDES** in the *History of the Peloponnesian War*, ca. 431 BC. Translation by Lionel Casson.

Surely oak and threefold brass surrounded his heart who first trusted a frail vessel to the merciless ocean...

HORACE from 'Odes', 23 BC

They change their clime, not their dispositions, who run across the sea.

HORACE from 'Odes', 23 BC

Give me a spirit that on this life's rough sea
Loves t'have his sails filled with a lusty wind,
Even till his sail-yards tremble, his masts crack,
And his rapt ship run on her side so low
That she drinks water, and her keel plows air.

> **GEORGE CHAPMAN** from *The Conspiracy of Charles, Duke of Byron*, 1608.
> Act III, scene I

He is an Otter, an Amphibium that lives both on Land and Water...his familiarity with death and danger, hath armed him with a kind of dissolute security against any encounter. The sea cannot roar more abroad, than hee within, fire him but with liquor... He makes small or no choice of his pallet; he can sleep as well on a Sacke of Pumice as a pillow of doune. He was never acquainted much with civilitie; the Sea has taught him other Rhetoricke... He can spin up a rope like a Spider, and down againe like a lightening. The rope is his roade, the topmast his Beacon...

> **RICHARD BRATHWAITE** from *Whimzies, or New Cast of Characters*, 1631

It has mistakenly been suggested that mariners are barbarous and incapable of leading more sensible and refined lives.

> **GEORGES FOURNIER** from *Hydrographie*, 1643

The qualities needed in a sailor are that he should be hardworking, trustworthy, attentive to himself and his duties, and reserved.

> **GEORGES FOURNIER** from *Hydrographie*, 1643

All you that would be seamen must bear a valiant heart.

> **MARTYN PARKER**

How little do the landsmen know
Of what we sailors feel,
When the waves do mount and winds do blow!
But we have hearts of steel!

> The Sailor's Resolution, 18th century

...the obstinacy of sailors is not always regulated by the importance of
the matter in dispute...

RICHARD WALTER from *A Voyage round the World by George Anson*, 1748

I observed in the behaviour of the sailors in this voyage, and on comparing it with what I have formerly seen of them at sea and on shore, I
am convinced that on land there is nothing more idle and dissolute; in
their own element there are no persons near the level of their degree
who live in the constant practice of half so many good qualities. They
are, for much the greater part, perfect masters of their business, and
always extremely alert, and ready in executing it, without any regard to
fatigue or hazard. The soldiers themselves are not better disciplined nor
more obedient to orders than these whilst aboard; they submit to every
difficulty which attends their calling with cheerfulness, and no less
virtues and patience and fortitude are exercised by them every day of
their lives.

All these good qualities, however, they always leave behind them on
shipboard; the sailor out of water is, indeed, as wretched an animal as
the fish out of water; for though the former hath, in common with
amphibious animals, the bare power of existing on land, yet if he be
kept there any time he never fails to become a nuisance.

HENRY FIELDING from *The Journal of a Voyage to Lisbon*, 1755

Seamen have always dwelt on the fringes of society. [Landsmen] were
familiar with seafarers only as the inhabitants of modern European
cities are familiar with tourists. They recognized their curious clothes
and eccentric behavior, they laughed at their oddities, they profited
from their ignorance—but they did not understand seamen, and they
knew nothing whatever of the world from which they came. Superfi-
cially familiar, the seaman remained to his contemporaries profoundly
strange. They knew him only on land, out of his element. The sailor on
a run ashore, probably drunk and riotous, was a popular image, but the
sailor afloat and at work was quite unfamiliar to his countrymen.

N. A. M. RODGER from *The Wooden World*, 1986. Rodger is describing
contemporary opinion of the British sailor in the middle of the 18th century.

Seamen were genuinely a peculiar class, isolated by their profession
from the bulk of their fellow-countrymen, living in particular quarters
of seaside towns, speaking in a language of their own, 'a people of a

distinct nature in themselves, for the most part divest of common knowledge of things ashore'. No analysis can do justice to them which attributes their actions simply to rational calculation. It would undoubtedly have been easier for sea officers to man and control their ships if seamen had been less turbulent and eccentric, but in practice that was the price to be paid for skill and daring.

> N. A. M. RODGER from *The Wooden World*, 1986. He is describing the British sailor of the mid-18th century.

Don't you see the ships a-coming?
  Don't you see them in full sail?
Don't you see the ships a-coming
  With the prizes at their tail?
 Oh! my little rolling sailor,
  Oh! my little rolling he;
I do love a jolly sailor,
  Blithe and merry might he be.

> Verses from a song sung by women in Gosport, England, in the late 18th century

No man will be a sailor who has contrivance enough to get himself into a jail; for being in a ship is being in a jail, with the chance of being drowned... A man in jail has more room, better food, and commonly better company.

> SAMUEL JOHNSON, 1759

When men come to like a sea-life, they are not fit to live on land.

> SAMUEL JOHNSON

For who are so free as the sons of the waves?

> DAVID GARRICK, 1759

The general Properties belonging to the common Mariner is to hand, reef, steer, knot and splice, with which Qualifications he may safely value himself upon the Calling of a good Seaman.

> A Naval Repository, 1762

...such are the tempers and disposissions of Seamen in general that whatever you give them out of the Common way although it be ever so much for their good yet it will not go down with them and you will hear nothing but murmurings gainest the man that first invented it; but the Moment they see their superiors set a Value upon it, it becomes the finest stuff in the World and the inventor a damn'd honest fellow.

> **CAPTAIN JAMES COOK**, 1769. Cook is writing about the reluctance of his crew to eat sauerkraut to prevent scurvy.

...sailors are, in fact, a different kind.

> **LORD BYRON** from the poem 'Don Juan', ca. 1824

There is not so helpless and pitiable an object in the world as a landsman beginning a sailor's life.

> **RICHARD HENRY DANA** from *Two Years Before the Mast*, 1840

A sailor has a peculiar cut to his clothes, and a way of wearing them which a green hand can never get.

> **RICHARD HENRY DANA** from *Two Years Before the Mast*, 1840

No man can be a sailor, or know what sailors are, unless he has lived in the forecastle with them—turned in and out with them, eaten of their dish and drank of their cup.

> **RICHARD HENRY DANA** from *Two Years Before the Mast*, 1840

...he was a true sailor, every finger a fish-hook.

> **RICHARD HENRY DANA** from *Two Years Before the Mast*, 1840

...a man is no sailor if he cannot sleep when he turns-in, and turn out when he's called.

> **RICHARD HENRY DANA** from *Two Years Before the Mast*, 1840

He is the best sailor who can steer within the fewest points of the wind, and exact a motive power out of the greatest obstacles.

> HENRY DAVID THOREAU from *A Week on the Concord and Merrimack Rivers*, 1849

...he had but little learning except what he had picked up from the sun and the sea.

> HERMAN MELVILLE from *Moby Dick*, 1851

...the wonder is always new that any sane man can be a sailor.

> RALPH WALDO EMERSON from *English Traits*, 1865

The power which the sea requires in a sailor makes a man of him very fast, and the change of shores and population clears his head of much nonsense of his wigwam.

> RALPH WALDO EMERSON

Frederick Weaver, who had shipped in the capacity of Able Seaman and Butcher, we find that he is utterly incompetent to perform the Duty of the former. He cannot Steer. He cannot Splice, and in fact he cannot do any thing regarding a Seaman's duty. He cannot even be trusted with a Lookout, not knowing a Cloud from a Ship. I therefore reduce his pay to Thirty Shillings a month.

> JOHN KYLE, Master of *Euterpe*, a British East Indiaman, April 17, 1869. *Euterpe*, renamed *Star of India*, is the oldest surviving steel-hulled sailing ship, and is on display at the San Diego Maritime Museum in San Diego, California.

Sailors are more like children than grown-up men, and require as much looking after. While there is water in the tanks, for instance, they will use it in the most extravagant manner, without thought for the morrow; and they are quite as reckless with their other stores.

> LADY ANNA BRASSEY's description of sailors from *A Voyage in the Sunbeam*, 1878

Home is the sailor, home from the sea.

> ROBERT LOUIS STEVENSON from the poem 'Requiem', 1887

It would be difficult to describe the subtle brotherhood of men that was here established on the seas.

STEPHEN CRANE from 'The Open Boat', 1897

...most seamen lead...a sedentary life. Their minds are of the stay-at-home order, and their home is always with them—the ship; so is their country—the sea.

JOSEPH CONRAD from *Heart of Darkness*, 1902

Oh, was there ever sailor free to choose,
That didn't settle somewhere near the sea?

RUDYARD KIPLING from the poem 'The Virginity', ca. 1903

Going to sea breeds a garrulous curiosity among sailors.

FELIX RIESENBERG

A day in the life of a sailor offers more adventure than the average man experiences in his entire lifetime.

CHARLES G. DAVIS

...I noticed how much at union with his boat this sailor was—stretched at ease, one arm thrown carelessly along the tiller, head just showing above the gunwale, and face uplifted so that his eyes commanded the luff of his sail.

ALFRED LOOMIS

The art of the sailor is to leave nothing to chance.

ANNIE VAN DE WIELE, small boat sailor

The professional seaman rarely turns to the sea for escape.

ALAN VILLIERS

With old sailors it was, and is, a matter of pride to be able to make knots, the more difficult and obscure, the better.

ALBERT RICHARD WETJEN

I have had to learn the simplest things last. Which made for difficulties. Even at sea I was slow, to get the hand out, or to cross a wet deck. The sea was not, finally, my trade.

CHARLES OLSON

Men in a ship are always looking up, and men ashore generally looking down.

JOHN MASEFIELD from *The Bird of Dawning*, 1933

If you wish to study ships, you must also study the men who sail them.

T. C. LETHBRIDGE

Sailors, with their built-in sense of order, service, and discipline, should really be running the world.

NICHOLAS MONSARRAT, 1966

A sailor's wonderfully handy about the house.

DOROTHY L. SAYERS

The brawling, boozy, semimoronic character one commonly meets in fiction, stumbling out of some dockside low-dive, has hardly ever shown up in real life—at least not in my lifetime of roaming the world.

TRISTAN JONES from *Yarns*, 1983

I have found that the average career seaman, of any grade, is on the whole more well read, and more expressive, than his shore-side counterparts.

TRISTAN JONES from *Yarns*, 1983

There are four kinds of seafarers under sail: dead; retired; novices; and pessimists.

TRISTAN JONES

You can't wring the seawater out of a sailor; it can't be done.

REAR ADMIRAL RONALD J. KURTH, U.S. Navy, 1989

As the miles bubble under the keel, sailors seem to shed skins one after the other until the scales so necessary for living in crowded cities and towns drop away, leaving just the human creature all but naked under the stars. For most, once those scales are gone, they never grow back quite as thick and hard as they once were.

GEORGE DAY from the article 'Sailing in Thin Water', 1990

There is no better company anywhere than men who love the sea.

JOHN LE CARRÉ from *The Secret Pilgrim*, 1991

A sailor is an artist whose medium is the wind.

WEBB CHILES

Sailor's Life

The seaman's story is of tempest...

SEXTUS PROPERTIUS from 'Elegies'

For when that we shall go to bed,
The pump is nigh our beddes head:
A man he were as good be dead
As smell thereof the stynke.

> 15th century English sea song. This verse is from the oldest known authentic English sea song. It refers to life onboard a merchant ship.

Item, that no blaspheming of God, or detestable swearing be used in any ship, nor communication of ribaldrie, filthy tales, or ungodly talke to be suffred in the company of any ship, neither dicing, carding, tabling, nor other divelish games to be frequented, whereby ensueth not onely povertie to the players, but also strife, variance, brauling, fighting, and oftentimes murther to the utter destruction of the parties...

    SEBASTIAN CABOT's Ordinances of 1553

For Sailors they be honest men,
And they do take great pains,
But Land-men and ruffling lads
Do rob them of their gains.

      16th century Elizabethan sea song

The stormy winds did blow,
And the raging seas did roar,
While we poor Sailors went to the tops,
And the land lubbers laid below.

      Chorus to 'The Mermaid', a 16th century Elizabethan sea song

...especially in fowle weather, then their labour, hazzard, wet, and cold, is so incredible I cannot expresse it... Men of all other professions in lightning, thunder, stormes, and tempests with raine and snow may shelter themselves in dry houses by good fires, but those are the chiefe times Sea-men must stand to their tackling, and attend with all diligence their greatest labour upon the deckes.

    CAPTAIN JOHN SMITH from *A Sea Grammar*, 1627

...at 4 PM had set weather foresail in doing which our men suffered extremely; the vessel frequently rolling them under water as they lay upon the yard; several of them were so benumbed as to be obliged to be helped in...

    PHILIP SAUMAREZ of the sloop *Tryal* describing the difficulties of rounding Cape Horn during Anson's circumnavigation, March 1741

...the ship, by labouring in this lofty sea, was now grown so loose in her upper works, that she let in the water at every seam, so that every part within board was constantly exposed to the sea-water, and scarcely any of the Officers ever lay in dry beds. Indeed it was very rare, that two nights ever passed without many of them being driven from their beds, by the deluge of water that came upon them.

> **RICHARD WALTER** from *A Voyage round the World by George Anson*, 1748. He describes the ship's passage through the Strait of Le Maire and rounding of Cape Horn in March 1741.

...we scraped our decks, and gave our ship a thorough cleansing; then smoked it between decks, and after all washed every part well with vinegar. These operations were extremely necessary for correcting the noisome stench on board, and destroying the vermin...

> **RICHARD WALTER** from *A Voyage round the World by George Anson*, 1748. Walter is describing the cleaning given to the flagship *Centurion* after arrival in Brazil from Madeira.

...the sick, who died apace on board, and doubtless the distemper was considerably augmented, by the stench and filthiness in which they lay; for the number of diseased was so great, and so few could be spared from the necessary duty of the sails to look after them, that it was impossible to avoid a great relaxation in the article of cleanliness, which had rendered the ship extremely loathsome between decks.

> **RICHARD WALTER** from *A Voyage round the World by George Anson*, 1748. Scurvy killed many men in Anson's crew, and he set up a recovery camp on Juan Fernández Island in June 1741.

...always took the greatest pleasure in keeping her clean in the highest degree, not even permitting the seamen to dine between decks when the weather would suffer them to eat above deck.

> Description of **ADMIRAL GEORGE RODNEY**'s penchant for cleanliness, ca. 1750

To anyone coming upon it for the first time, the life of a ship was extraordinary. On first being 'registered in a wooden world', one entered a peculiar society, with its own manners, dress and language, all equally unexpected to an outsider.

> **N. A. M. RODGER** from *The Wooden World*, 1986. Rodger is writing about life in the English Navy in the mid-1700s.

I have observed too, whenever ye get any money paid, ye do not act with it like rational creatures and lay it out on clothes and necessaries, but ye throw it immediately away on dirty whores and in stinking gin.

> **CAPTAIN EDWARD WHEELER**, Royal Navy, speaking to his crew in 1760

...beg leave to represent our hard case on board this vessel where there is not the least conveniency for the number of men on board, not having room to eat our victuals below, but is obliged to mess upon the open deck in all weathers, and great part of us are glad to lie on the cables and casks, though as many as can turn in and out two in a hammock; and when we are at sea, if it blows but a reef in the topsails, the hatches are obliged to be battened down and then we are glad to fly to the boats to eat our provisions; and when we go off the deck to our rest we are obliged to strip our clothes off before we go down, let it blow or rain ever so, and then to creep on our hands and knees to our hammocks, and we are almost devoured with vermin by stowing two in a hammock and so close, not having more room for two than is allowed for a single man.

> Petition by the crew of *Flamborough's Prize*, asking the Admiralty for a different ship, 1761

I thought sailors must be happy men to have such opportunities of visiting foreign countries and beholding the wonderful works of the Creator in the remote regions of the earth; I thought of nothing but pleasant gales and prosperous voyages.

> **WILLIAM SPAVENS**, ca. 1796

Our clothes were all wet through, and the only change was from wet to more wet.

> **RICHARD HENRY DANA** from *Two Years Before the Mast*, 1840. No sailor remained dry on a sailing ship rounding Cape Horn.

It is the officers' duty to keep every one at work, even if there is nothing to be done but to scrape the rust from the chain cables. In no state prison are the convicts more regularly set to work, or more closely watched.

RICHARD HENRY DANA from *Two Years Before the Mast*, 1840

A song is as necessary to sailors as the drum and fife to a soldier. They can't pull in time, or pull with a will, without it.

RICHARD HENRY DANA from *Two Years Before the Mast*, 1840

Bad weather and hard work at sea can be borne up against very well, if only one has spirit and health; but there is nothing brings a man down...like bodily pain and want of sleep.

RICHARD HENRY DANA from *Two Years Before the Mast*, 1840

A sailor is always presumed to be well, and if he's sick, he's a poor dog. One has to stand his wheel, and another his lookout, and the sooner he gets on deck again, the better.

RICHARD HENRY DANA from *Two Years Before the Mast*, 1840

Oh, times is hard and the wages low
It's time for us to roll and go.

Chantey 'Round the Bay of Mexico'

And now the storm is over,
And we are safe and well;
We will walk into a public house
And drink and drink our fill;
We will drink strong ale and porter,
And we'll make the rafters roar,
And when our money is all spent
We'll be off to sea once more!

Liverpool halyard chantey 'The Holy Ground'. The Holy Ground referred to a brothel located on land owned by the church.

When your money's gone
It's the same old song,
Get up Jack! John sit down!

  Chantey 'Jolly Roving Tar'

Gustave Lime A.B. while stowing the fore top gallant Sail, fell from the yard overboard, and was lost, the night being dark and squally with a strong chop sea it was impossible to get a boat out without a very great risk of losing the boat and crew.

  WILLIAM COSENS, Master of *Euterpe*, a British East Indiaman, April 17, 1869

The sheets were frozen hard, and they cut the naked hand;
The decks were like a slide, where a seaman scarce could stand;
The wind was a nor'wester, blowing squally off the sea;
And cliffs and spouting breakers were the only things a-lee.

  ROBERT LOUIS STEVENSON from the poem 'Christmas at Sea'

I remember a few nights in my lifetime, and in a big ship, too, when one did not get flung out of one's bed simply because one never even attempted to get in; one had been too weary, too hopeless to try.

  JOSEPH CONRAD from *The Mirror of the Sea*, 1906

When we were down below in the half-deck, the little room twelve feet square, where the six boys lived and slept, we were almost happy. We had rigged up a bogey stove, with a chimney which kinked into elbows whenever the roll was very heavy. It did not burn very well, this bogey stove, but we contrived to cook by it... It was our great delight to sit upon our chests in the dog watch, looking at the bogey, listening to the creaking chimney, watching the smoke pouring out from the chinks. In the night watches, when the sleepers lay quiet in their bunks behind the red baize curtains, one or two of us who kept the deck would creep below to put on coal. That was the golden time, the time of the night watch, to sit there in the darkness among the sleepers hearing the coals click.

  JOHN MASEFIELD from *A Tarpaulin Muster*, 1907. Masefield is writing about rounding Cape Horn in a sailing ship.

I have had to pass a considerable portion of my life aboard small craft of various kinds, and after a long and mixed experience of the life, I have come to two very definite conclusions concerning it. One is that life on a small boat in fine weather is the only kind of life worth living. The other is that, in bad weather, it's just plain hell.

WESTON MARTYR from *The Southseasman*, 1926

At first we shivered when an icy finger of water found its way down our backs or up a sleeve, but soon we were so wet and so cold we ceased to care. Get wet and stay wet is the best policy for sailing ships. The greatest agony of mind comes when you change into comparative dry, only to know with horrible certainty that as soon as you go on deck again everything will be sodden once more...

RONALD WALKER from *Men Ships and the Sea* by Alan Villiers, 1973. Walker and Villiers shipped aboard the three-masted square rigger *Grace Harwar* to make a film about sailing ships. Walker's diary entry describes conditions off the coast of New Zealand in May 1929. He died shortly thereafter in an accident aloft. He had been at sea only two months; his death added to the *Grace Harwar*'s reputation as a mankiller.

We were cold. There is no heating system in a full-rigged ship. The very cockroaches retired from active service and might all have died for all we saw of them.

ALAN VILLIERS from *Men Ships and the Sea*, 1973. He is describing the passage of the three-masted square rigger *Grace Harwar* off the coast of New Zealand in 1929.

When the wind returned it was from the east again, with fog, rain, and gale in succession. Oilskins were useless. There was no dry spot in the ship, nor a dry rag to wear. The forecastle was washed out time and time again. When the forecastle doors were shut, the air was stifling. When they were open, great seas swept joyously in. We kept them shut, preferring suffocation to exposure.

ALAN VILLIERS from *Men Ships and the Sea*, 1973. Bad weather plagued the three-masted square rigger *Grace Harwar* as she attempted to pass through Cook Strait between North Island and South Island in New Zealand in 1929.

Sailors' Thoughts

Hope has no role at sea.

    Anonymous

If a man does not know to what port he is steering, no wind is favorable to him.

    SENECA

When one has good wine,
A graceful junk,
And a maiden's love,
Why envy the immortal gods?

    LI PO

Nathless there knocketh now
The heart's thought that I on high streams
The salt-wavy tumult traverse alone.
Moaneth alway my mind's lust
That I fare forth, that I afar hence
Seek out a foreign fastness.

    'The Seafarer', a 10th century Anglo-Saxon poem. Translation by Ezra Pound.

Of course I am lonely at sea, but one suffers less on the ocean in that respect than in the heart of London.

    SIR WALTER RALEIGH

He who goes to sea for pleasure would go to Hell for a pastime.

    SAMUEL JOHNSON

Alone, alone, all, all alone,
Alone on a wide wide sea!
And never a saint took pity on
My soul in agony.

    SAMUEL TAYLOR COLERIDGE from the poem 'The Rime of the Ancient Mariner', 1798

Ay, ay! we sailors sail not in vain. We expatriate ourselves to nationalize with the universe; and in all our voyages round the world, we are still accompanied by those old circumnavigators, the stars, who are shipmates and fellow-sailors of ours—sailing in heaven's blue, as we on the azure main. Let genteel generations scoff at our hardened hands, and finger-nails tipped with tar—did they ever clasp truer palms than ours? Let them feel of our sturdy hearts, beating like sledge-hammers in those hot smithies, our bosoms; with their amber-headed canes, let them feel of our generous pulses, and swear that they go off like thirty-two pounders.

HERMAN MELVILLE from *White-Jacket*, 1850

Whenever I find myself growing grim about the mouth; whenever it is a damp, drizzly November in my soul; whenever I find myself involuntarily pausing before coffin warehouses, and bringing up the rear of every funeral I meet; and especially whenever my hypos get such an upper hand of me, that it requires a strong moral principle to prevent myself from deliberately stepping into the street, and knocking people's hats off—then I account it high time to get to sea as soon as I can.

HERMAN MELVILLE from *Moby Dick*, 1851. The speaker is Ishmael.

Sea of the brine of life and of unshovell'd yet always-ready graves...

WALT WHITMAN from the poem 'Song of Myself', 1855

I remember the black wharves and the slips,
And the sea-tides tossing free;
And Spanish sailors with bearded lips,
And the beauty and majesty of the ships,
And the magic of the sea.

HENRY WADSWORTH LONGFELLOW from the poem 'My Lost Youth', 1858

And though thy soul sail leagues and leagues
        beyond—
Still, leagues beyond those leagues, there is more
        sea.

DANTE GABRIEL ROSSETTI from the poem 'Sonnets from the House of Life', ca. 1870

There is nothing so desperately monotonous as the sea, and I no longer wonder at the cruelty of pirates.

    JAMES RUSSELL LOWELL

Exultation is the going
Of an inland soul to sea...

    EMILY DICKINSON from the poem 'Exultation is the going', 1890

Nothing is more dreadful to the mind of a sailor, I think, than a possible encounter with a hungry shark.

    JOSHUA SLOCUM from *Sailing Alone Around the World*, 1900

The days passed happily with me wherever my ship sailed.

    JOSHUA SLOCUM from *Sailing Alone Around the World*, 1900

Nowhere else than upon the sea do the days, weeks and months fall away quicker into the past.

    JOSEPH CONRAD from *The Mirror of the Sea*, 1906

But of the delight of seeing a small craft run bravely amongst the great seas there can be no question to him whose soul does not dwell ashore.

    JOSEPH CONRAD from *The Mirror of the Sea*, 1906

I feel homesick for the sea, the desire to look again on the level expanse of salt water which has so often lulled me, which has smiled at me so frequently under the sparkling sunshine of a lovely day, which many times too has hurled the threat of death in my face with a swirl of white foam whipped by the wind under the dark December sky...

    JOSEPH CONRAD

To touch that bow is to rest one's hand on the cosmic nose of things.

    JACK LONDON from *The Cruise of the Snark*, 1911

...I notice the stars being blotted out. Walls of darkness close in upon me, so that when the last star is gone, the darkness is so near that it seems I can reach out and touch it on every side. When I lean toward it, I can feel it loom against my face.

> **JACK LONDON** from *The Cruise of the Snark*, 1911

The sea is at its best at London, near midnight, when you are within the arms of a capacious chair, before a glowing fire, selecting phases of the voyages you will never make.

> **H. M. TOMLINSON** from *The Sea and the Jungle*, 1913

Most of us, I suppose, are a little nervous of the sea. No matter what its smiles may be, we doubt its friendship.

> **H. M. TOMLINSON**

The sea folds away from you like a mystery.

> **CARL SANDBURG**

I honestly confess that many times, when I saw my sails in ribbons and my poor boat struggling separately on a raging sea, plunging down terrific precipices, disappearing under monstrous waves that threatened to swallow her, then pointing her bows to the black skies as if to implore the mercy of Him whose will disposes life and death, yes, many times I said to myself: 'If I get away with it this time, I'll never set foot on a boat again'.

> **MARCEL BARDIAUX**

The truth is I hate motors on a sailing ship. I resent them and therefore I neglect them.

> **SIR FRANCIS CHICHESTER**

To me, nothing made by man is more beautiful than a sailboat under way in fine weather, and to be *on* that sailboat is to be as close to heaven as I expect to get.

> **ROBERT MANRY.** In 1965 he crossed the Atlantic from the United States to England in *Tinkerbelle*, a 13.5-foot sloop, the smallest sailboat to successfully make the voyage.

Round the world goes further than the ends of the earth, as far as life itself, perhaps further still. When you sense that, your head begins to swim, you are a little afraid.

Circumnavigator **BERNARD MOITESSIER**

I feel passing through my whole being that breath of the high seas that once felt is never forgotten.

BERNARD MOITESSIER

You long for port, although at the very end you are never quite sure whether it is the delight of the landfall or regret that the voyage is done...but underneath it all you know that what is troubling you is that your goal has been achieved and is gone.

WILLIAM A. ROBINSON from *Return to the Sea*

I can't wait for the oil wells to run dry, for the last gob of black, sticky muck to come oozing out of some remote well. Then the glory of sail will return.

TRISTAN JONES from *Ice!*, 1978

Being alone is not the same thing as being lonely. I can feel more lonely on the New York subway than I ever would in mid-Atlantic... I have felt closer to people while alone in midocean than I sometimes have felt whilst being in the same room with them.

TRISTAN JONES from *Yarns*, 1983

Night closed us in gently and we lit the kerosene running lamps and hung them in the rigging. Out there in the middle of nowhere they looked cheerful and secure. I felt as if everything bad in my life had remained onshore and everything good was out on the water with me.

BOB SHACOCHIS from 'Dead Reckoning', a short story in *Easy in the Islands*, 1985

For those who can meet the demands of sea and weather, the boatman's life can be unhurried and footloose, the opposite of the rat race.

TOM WICKER from 'Rough Passage', 1988

What the hell were we doing here, hundreds of miles from land, with our lives in constant peril, out of contact with the world. I thought of my mother. She can't swim a stroke and is scared to death of the water. How could it be that her son, flesh of her flesh, would choose a life that placed him and his mate in the middle of the Tasman Sea in a violent storm with only a thin skin of fiberglass between them and a watery grave?

JIM MOORE from *By Way of the Wind*, 1991

If you can't repair it, maybe it shouldn't be on board.

LIN and **LARRY PARDEY**

... like a blind sailor remembering the sea...

JAMES SALTER from *Burning the Days*, 1997

Sails

But soon an offshore breeze blew to our liking, a canvas-bellying breeze... The bows went plunging...sails cracked and lashed out.

HOMER from *The Odyssey*, ca. 700 BC

One night, while we were in these tropics, I went out to the end of the flying-jib boom, upon some duty, and, having finished it, turned round, and lay over the boom for a long time, admiring the beauty of the sight before me...there rose up from the water, supported only by the small black hull, a pyramid of canvas, spreading out far beyond the hull, and towering up almost, as it seemed in the indistinct night air, to the clouds... So quiet, too, was the sea, and so steady the breeze, that if these sails had been sculptured marble, they could not have been more motionless. Not a ripple upon the surface of the canvas; not even a

quivering of the extreme edges of the sail—so perfectly were they
distended by the breeze. I was so lost in the sight, that I forgot the
presence of the man who came out with me, until he said, (for he, too,
rough old man-of-war's man as he was, had been gazing at the show)
half to himself, still looking at the marble sails—'How quietly they do
their work!'

        RICHARD HENRY DANA from *Two Years Before the Mast*, 1840

The sail bends gently to the breeze, as swells some generous impulse of
the heart, and anon flutters and flaps with a kind of human suspense. I
could watch the motions of a sail forever, they are so rich and full of
meaning. I watch the play of its pulse, as if it were my own blood
beating there.

        HENRY DAVID THOREAU from *Journals*, 1840

It is a free, buoyant creature, the bauble of the heavens and the earth. A
gay pastime the air plays with it. If it wells and tugs, it is because the
sun lays his windy finger on it. The breeze it plays with has been
outdoors so long. So thin is it, and yet so full of life; so noiseless when it
labors hardest, so noisy and impatient when least serviceable.

        HENRY DAVID THOREAU from *Journals*, 1840

The north wind stepped readily into the harness which we had provided, and pulled us along with good will. Sometimes we sailed as
gently and steadily as the clouds overhead...

        HENRY DAVID THOREAU

I have spliced my old sail to a new one, and now go out to try it in a sail
to Baker's Farm. I like it much. It pulls like an ox and makes me think
there's more wind abroad than there is.

        HENRY DAVID THOREAU from *Journals*, 1858

Many people develop a kind of love-hate relationship with the spinnaker, and it has often been said that this sail is the easiest to hoist but
requires the most courage.

        R. 'BUNTY' KING from *Spinnaker*, 1981

When the schooner yacht *America*, racing in 1851 against the largest and fastest British yachts, beat the fleet and won the cup which for all time bears her name, she proved, among other things, the importance of well shaped sails for making a yacht go fast. The *America*'s sails were made of cotton, while the British yachts' sails were flax. The cotton sails retained their shape far better than the flax ones which were prone to bag and bulge in the wrong places.

> **BOB BAVIER** from *Sailing to Win*, 1983

If every sailmaker would stop looking at the inside of the sails and start paying attention to the back side, he'd have a much better idea of what Mother Nature sees.

> **BUDDY MELGES**, 1994

Science

Those who wish to study sea life—and there is much to be done in this field—should travel by tramp steamers, or, better still, sailing vessels.

> **APSLEY CHERRY-GERRARD** from *The Worst Journey in the World*, 1922

Scurvy

And by reason of the long navigation, and want of food and water, they fall into sundry diseases, their gummes waxe great, and swell, and they are faine to cut them away, their legges swell, and all the body becommeth sore, and so benummed, that they can not stirre hand nor foot, and so they die for weakenesse, others fall into fluxes and agues, and die thereby.

> **THOMAS STEVENS**, 1579. Stevens sailed from Lisbon to Goa in a Portuguese ship.

The sensitiveness of the bodies of these sick people is so great that...the best aid which can be rendered them is not even to touch the bedclothes...the upper and lower gums of the mouth in the inside of the mouth and outside the teeth, become swollen to such a size that neither the teeth nor the molars can be brought together. The teeth become so loose and without support that they move while moving the head... With this they cannot eat anything but food in liquid form or drinks...they come to be so weakened in this condition that their natural vigor fails them, and they die all of a sudden, while talking.

ANTONIO DE LA ASCENSION, a Spanish monk, who first accurately described scurvy, 1602

I shall endeavour to remove a very great prejudice from which persons who labour under this affliction have been most unjustly suffered which is that none but the indolent are ever sick of this disease. This mistaken opinion has caused many poor sufferers to endure more from their commanding officers than from the distemper itself; being drubbed to do their duty, when incapable of it. Our experience has abundantly testified that the most active, stirring persons are oftenest seized with this disease; and the continuation of their labour only helps to kill them the sooner.

Member of the Anson circumnavigation, 1740–1744

Soon after our passing Streights Le Maire, the scurvy began to make its appearance amongst us...at the latter end of April there were but a few on board, who were not in some degree afflicted with it, and in that month no less than forty-three died of it on board the *Centurion*...in the month of May we lost near double that number: And as we did not get to land till the middle of June, the mortality went on increasing, and the disease extended itself so prodigiously, that after the loss of above two hundred men, we could not at last muster more than six fore-mast men in a watch capable of duty.

RICHARD WALTER from *A Voyage round the World by George Anson*, 1748. Walter is describing conditions on board the flagship *Centurion* after rounding Cape Horn in 1741.

This disease so frequently attending all long voyages, and so particularly destructive to us, is surely the most singular and unaccountable of any that affects the human body. For its symptoms are inconstant and innumerable, and its progress and effects extremely irregular...yet there are some symptoms which are more general than the rest... These common appearances are large discoloured spots dispersed over the whole surface of the body, swelled legs, putrid gums, and above all, an extraordinary lassitude of the whole body, especially after any exercise, however inconsiderable.

> **RICHARD WALTER** from *A Voyage round the World by George Anson*, 1748

But notwithstanding this plenty of water, and that the fresh provisions were distributed amongst the sick, and the whole crew fed often upon fish, yet neither were the sick hereby relieved, nor the progress and advancement of the disease retarded: Nor was it in these instances only that we found ourselves disappointed; for though it has been usually esteemed a necessary piece of management to keep all ships, where the crews are large, as clean and airy between decks as possible; and it hath been believed by many, that this particular, if well attended to, would prevent the appearance of scurvy, or at least, mitigate its effects; yet we observed, during the latter part of our run, that though we kept all our ports open, and took uncommon pains in cleansing and sweetening the ships, yet neither the progress, nor the virulence of the disease were thereby sensibly abated.

> **RICHARD WALTER** from *A Voyage round the World by George Anson*, 1748.
> Scurvy became widespread on Anson's *Centurion* during a fourteen-week crossing of the Pacific in 1742.

This disease is not so common now as formerly; and is attributed generally to salt provisions, want of cleanliness, the free use of grease and fat, and, last of all, to laziness.

> **RICHARD HENRY DANA** from *Two Years Before the Mast*, 1840

The Sea

In the beginning God created the heaven and the earth. And the earth was without form, and void; and darkness was upon the face of the deep. And the Spirit of God moved upon the face of the water.

> The Holy Bible, King James Version, Genesis 1:1-2

Water can both float and sink a ship.

> Chinese proverb

All streams run to the sea, but the sea is not full.

> The Holy Bible, Revised Standard Version, Ecclesiastes 1:7

The sea is His, for He made it.

> The Holy Bible, Revised Standard Version, Psalms 95:5

Yonder is the sea, great and wide,
which teems with things innumerable,
living things both small and great.

> The Holy Bible, Revised Standard Version, Psalms 104:25

The sea washed away all mortal evils.

> **EURIPIDES** from *Iphigenia in Tauris*

Nothing is so sweet as to return from sea and listen to the raindrops on
the rooftops of home.

> **SOPHOCLES**

Every part of the sea is dangerous.

> **ANTIPATER** of Thessalonica

Pleasant it is, when over a great sea the winds trouble the waters, to
gaze from shore upon another's great tribulations: not because any
man's troubles are a delectable joy, but because to perceive what ills
you are free from yourself is pleasant.

> **LUCRETIUS** from *De Rerum Natura* (*On the Nature of Things*), ca. 70 BC

Never trust her at any time when the calm sea shows her false alluring
smile.

> **LUCRETIUS** from *De Rerum Natura* (*On the Nature of Things*), ca. 70 BC

Beyond all things is the ocean.

SENECA

The profit of the sea would be good if there were no fear of waves.

SAADI (Sheikh Muslih-uddin Saadi Shirazi) from 'The Gulistan of Saadi', 1258

...this bloody ocean, seething like a pot on a hot fire.

CHRISTOPHER COLUMBUS, 1492

Praise the sea; on shore remain.

JOHN FLORIO from *Second Frutes*, 1591

The sea being smooth
How many shallow bauble boats dare sail
Upon her patient breast...

WILLIAM SHAKESPEARE from *Troilus and Cressida*, 1603. Speech of Nestor, act I, scene III.

As God hath combined the Sea and Land into one Globe, so their joynt combination and mutuall assistance is necessary to Secular happinesse and glory. The Sea covereth one halfe of this patrimony of Man... Thus should Man at once lose halfe his Inheritance, if the Art of Navigation did not inable him to manage this untamed Beast, and with the Bridle of the Winds, and Saddle of his Shipping to make him serviceable.

SAMUEL PURCHAS from *Purchas His Pilgrimes*, 1625

...of all objects that I have ever seen, there is none which affects my imagination so much as the sea or ocean.

JOSEPH ADDISON from an essay on the sea in the *Spectator*, 1712

The ocean is an object of no small terror.

EDMUND BURKE from 'On the Sublime and Beautiful', 1757

Neither nature nor art has partitioned the sea into empires. The ocean and its treasures are the common property of all men.

JOHN ADAMS

The gentleness of heaven broods o'er the Sea.

WILLIAM WORDSWORTH from the poem 'It is a beauteous evening, calm and free', 1802

...the sea, where every maw
The greater on the less feeds evermore...

JOHN KEATS

There is a rapture on the lonely shore,
There is society, where none intrudes,
By the deep Sea, and music in its roar.

LORD BYRON from the poem 'Childe Harold's Pilgrimage', 1818

Roll on, thou deep and dark-blue Ocean—roll!
Ten thousand fleets sweep over thee in vain;
Man marks the earth with ruin—his control
Stops with the shore;—upon the watery plain
The wrecks are all thy deed, nor doth remain
A shadow of man's ravage...

LORD BYRON from the poem 'Childe Harold's Pilgrimage', 1818

And I have loved thee, Ocean! and my joy
Of youthful sports was on thy breast to be
Borne like thy bubbles, onward: from a boy
I wanton'd with thy breakers,—they to me
Were a delight; and if the freshening sea
Made them a terror—'twas a pleasing fear,
For I was as it were a child of thee,
And trusted to thy billows far and near,
And laid my hand upon thy mane—as I do here.

LORD BYRON from the poem 'Childe Harold's Pilgrimage', 1818

While sailing a little south of the Plata on one very dark night, the sea presented a wonderful and most beautiful spectacle. There was a fresh breeze, and every part of the surface, which during the day is seen as foam, now glowed with a pale light. The vessel drove before her bows two billows of liquid phosphorous, and in her wake she was followed by a milky train. As far as the eye reached, the crest of every wave was bright, and the sky above the horizon, from the reflected glare of these livid flames, was not so utterly obscure as over the vault of heaven.

CHARLES DARWIN from *The Voyage of the Beagle*, 1839

And what are the boasted glories of the illimitable ocean? A tedious waste, a desert of water, as the Arabian calls it.

CHARLES DARWIN

There is a witchery in the sea, its songs and stories, and in the mere sight of a ship, and the sailor's dress, especially to a young mind, which has done more to man navies, and fill merchantmen, than all the press-gangs of Europe.

RICHARD HENRY DANA from *Two Years Before the Mast*, 1840

...nothing will compare with the early breaking of day upon the wide ocean.

RICHARD HENRY DANA from *Two Years Before the Mast*, 1840

The sea heaves up, hangs loaded o'er the land,
Breaks there and buries its tumultuous strength.

ROBERT BROWNING

Now, in calm weather, to swim in the open ocean is as easy to the practiced swimmer as to ride in a spring-carriage ashore. But the awful lonesomeness is intolerable. The intense concentration of self in the middle of such a heartless immensity, my God! who can tell it?

HERMAN MELVILLE from *Moby Dick*, 1851

There is, one knows not what sweet mystery about this sea, whose
gentle awful stirrings seem to speak of some hidden soul beneath.

HERMAN MELVILLE

The wonders of the sea are as marvelous as the glories of the heavens;
and they proclaim, in songs divine, that they too are the work of holy
fingers.

MATTHEW FONTAINE MAURY from *The Physical Geography of the Sea*, 1855

Sea of stretch'd ground swells,
Sea breathing broad and convulsive breaths,
Sea of the brine of life and of unshovell'd yet always-ready graves,
Howler and scooper of storms, capricious and dainty sea,
I am integral with you, I too am of one phase and of all phases.

WALT WHITMAN from the poem 'Song of Myself' from *Leaves of Grass*, 1855

The sea remembers nothing. It is feline. It licks your feet—its huge
flanks purr very pleasantly for you; but it will crack your bones and eat
you, for all that, and wipe the crimson foam from its jaws as if nothing
had happened.

OLIVER WENDELL HOLMES from *The Autocrat of the Breakfast-Table*, 1858

The sea drowns out humanity and time; it has no sympathy with either,
for it belongs to eternity, and of that it sings its monotonous song for
ever and ever.

OLIVER WENDELL HOLMES from *The Autocrat of the Breakfast-Table*, 1858

To me the sea is a continual miracle,
The fishes that swim—the rocks
—the motion of the waves
—the ships with men in them,
What stranger miracles are there?

WALT WHITMAN from the poem 'Miracles' from *Leaves of Grass*, 1860

The Sea never has been, and I fancy never will be nor can be, painted; it is only suggested by means of more or less spiritual and intelligent conventionalism.

JOHN RUSKIN

All the earth's full rivers cannot fill
The sea, that drinking, thirsteth still.

CHRISTINA ROSSETTI from the poem 'By the Sea', 1862

We do not associate the idea of antiquity with the ocean, nor wonder how it looked a thousand years ago as we do of the land, for it was equally wild and unfathomable always.

HENRY DAVID THOREAU from *Cape Cod*, 1865

The restless ocean may at any moment cast up a whale or a wrecked vessel at your feet.

HENRY DAVID THOREAU from *Cape Cod*, 1865

The ocean is a wilderness reaching round the globe, wilder than a Bengal jungle, and fuller of monsters, washing the very wharves of our cities and the gardens of our sea-side residences.

HENRY DAVID THOREAU from *Cape Cod*, 1865

The sea is masculine, the type of active strength. Look, what egg-shells are drifting all over it, each one, like ours, filled with men in ecstasies of terror, alternating with cockney conceit, as the sea is rough or smooth.

RALPH WALDO EMERSON from *English Traits*, 1865

I will go back to the great sweet mother
Mother and lover of men, the sea.

ALGERNON CHARLES SWINBURNE from the poem 'The Triumph of Time', 1866

How the water sports and sings! (surely it is alive!)

WALT WHITMAN from the poem 'Song at Sunset' from *Leaves of Grass*,
ca. 1875

Who can say of a particular sea that it is old? Distilled by the sun,
kneaded by the moon, it is renewed in a year, in a day, or in an hour.

THOMAS HARDY from *The Return of the Native*, 1878

The first and most obvious light in which the sea presents itself from
the political and social viewpoint is that of a great highway; or better,
perhaps, of a wide common, over which all men may pass in all directions.

ALFRED THAYER MAHAN from *The Influence of Seapower Upon History*, 1890

The voice of the sea speaks to the soul. The touch of the sea is sensuous,
enfolding the body in its soft, close embrace.

KATE CHOPIN from *The Awakening*, 1899

I once knew a writer who, after saying beautiful things about the sea,
passed through a Pacific hurricane, and he became a changed man.

JOSHUA SLOCUM from *Sailing Alone Around the World*, 1900

Who hath desired the Sea?—the sight of salt water unbounded—
The heave and the halt and the hurl and the crash of the comber
    wind-hounded?

RUDYARD KIPLING from the poem 'The Sea and the Hills', 1902

The sea never changes and its works, for all the talk of men, are
wrapped in mystery.

JOSEPH CONRAD from *Falk*, 1903

I have known the sea too long to believe in its respect for decency.

JOSEPH CONRAD from *Falk*, 1903

...the sea has never been friendly to man... He—man or people—who, putting his trust in the friendship of the sea, neglects the strength and cunning of his right hand, is a fool! As if it were too great, too mighty for common virtues, the ocean has no compassion, no faith, no law, no memory. Its fickleness is to be held true to men's purposes only by an undaunted resolution, and by a sleepless, armed, jealous vigilance, in which, perhaps, there has always been more hate than love.

JOSEPH CONRAD from *The Mirror of the Sea*, 1906

Impenetrable and heartless, the sea has given nothing of itself to the suitors for its precarious favors. Unlike the earth, it cannot be subjugated at any cost of patience and toil.

JOSEPH CONRAD from *The Mirror of the Sea*, 1906

And I looked upon the true sea—the sea that plays with men till their hearts are broken, and wears stout ships to death. Nothing can touch the brooding bitterness of its soul. Open to all and faithful to none, it exercises its fascination for the undoing of the best. To love it is not well.

JOSEPH CONRAD from *The Mirror of the Sea*, 1906

And now the old ships and their men are gone; the new ships and the new men, many of them bearing the old auspicious names, have taken up their watch on the stern and impartial sea, which offers no opportunities but to those who know how to grasp them with a ready hand and undaunted heart.

JOSEPH CONRAD from *The Mirror of the Sea*, 1906

The sea—this truth must be confessed—has no generosity.

JOSEPH CONRAD from *The Mirror of the Sea*, 1906

The most amazing wonder of the deep is its unfathomable cruelty.

JOSEPH CONRAD from *The Mirror of the Sea*, 1906

The sea is the great disturber. Nothing human can endure for long unchanged in its presence.

FILSON YOUNG

Everything can be found at sea according to the spirit of your quest.

JOSEPH CONRAD from *Some Reminiscences*, later re-titled *A Personal Record*, 1912

Twas them days a ship was part of the sea, and a man was part of the ship, and the sea joined all together and made it one.

EUGENE O'NEILL from *The Hairy Ape*, 1922

The sea, like a great sultan, supports thousands of ships, his lawful wives.

FELIX REISENBERG

The sea is always the same: and yet the sea always changes.

CARL SANDBURG from the poem 'North Atlantic'

The seas are the heart's blood of the earth... The rhythm of waves beats in the sea like a pulse in living flesh. It is pure force, forever embodying itself in a succession of watery shapes which vanish on its passing.

HENRY BESTON from *The Outermost House*, 1928

Only in its endless variety is the sea unchanging. It is always the same, and it is never the same.

ALBERT RICHARD WETJEN from *Way for a Sailor!*, 1931

At the last, when you have sailed long enough and far enough, you come to understand that the sea is everything. It is calm and restless, stormy and laughing, many-hued and one-colored, salty and fresh, warm and cold, an enemy and a friend, a help and a hindrance, a tragedy and a jest. Everything!

ALBERT RICHARD WETJEN from *Way for a Sailor!*, 1931

Watching it, as we rocked over its heaving waters, the sea became for me the All-Mother, the watery womb that produced the first life, the moon, the eternal female.

DORA BIRTLES from *North-West by North*, 1935

...the sea is the same as it has been since before men ever went on it in boats.

ERNEST HEMINGWAY

The cure for anything is saltwater—sweat, tears, or the sea.

ISAK DINESEN

The ocean is a place of paradoxes.

RACHEL CARSON from *Under Sea*, 1937

To the small boat voyager it is the sea which comes first: it is the supreme consideration, stretching to every shore, wind-cut and passionate, greater in breadth and loneliness, than all the deserts of the world together.

RICHARD MAURY

The sea is the land's edge also, the granite
Into which it reaches, the beaches where it tosses
Its hints of earlier and other creation:
The starfish, the horseshoe crab, the whale's backbone;
The pools where it offers to our curiosity
The more delicate algae and the sea anemone.
It tosses up our losses, the torn seine,
The shattered lobster pot, the broken oar
And the fear of foreign dead men. The sea has
    many voices.

T. S. ELIOT from the poem 'The Dry Salvages', 1941

The sea lolls, laps and idles in, with fishes sleeping in its lap.

DYLAN THOMAS

No man who loves the sea can ever know peace unless he can look out over water, even if from the shore.

CARLETON MITCHELL from *Islands to Windward*, 1948

The sea, in fact, is that state of barbaric vagueness and disorder out of which civilisation has emerged and into which, unless saved by the effort of gods and men, it is always liable to relapse.

W. H. AUDEN

In the moods and the silences of a great ocean there lies an uncertainty, like a question mark, that is the reflection of life itself.

PETER PYE

Because I spend a lot of time sailing, people often say to me, 'How you must love the sea.' I don't love the sea and I don't believe that anybody does. Of course one admires it, respects it, and speaking for myself, often fears and sometimes hates it; but love it, never.

ERIC HISCOCK

...the sea lies all about us. The commerce of all lands must cross it. The very winds that move over the lands have been cradled on its broad expanse and seek ever to return to it. The continents themselves dissolve and pass to the sea, in grain after grain of eroded land. So the rains that rose from it return again in rivers. In its mysterious past it encompasses all the dim origins of life and receives in the end, after, it may be, many transmutations, the dead husks of that same life. For all at last return to the sea—to Oceanus, the ocean river, like the ever-flowing stream of time, the beginning and the end.

RACHEL CARSON from *The Sea Around Us*, 1951

Beginnings are apt to be shadowy, and so it is with the beginnings of that great mother of life, the sea.

RACHEL CARSON from *The Sea Around Us*, 1951

Who has known the ocean? Neither you nor I, with our earth-bound senses, know the foam and surge of the tide...

RACHEL CARSON

He always thought of the sea as la mar which is what people call her in
Spanish when they love her. Sometimes those who love her say bad
things of her but they are always said as though she were a woman...the
old man always thought of her as feminine and as something that gave
or withheld great favors, and if she did wild or wicked things it was
because she could not help them.

> **ERNEST HEMINGWAY** from *The Old Man and the Sea*, 1952

The ocean knows no favorites. Her bounty is reserved for those who
have the wit to learn her secrets, the courage to bear her buffets, and the
will to persist... in her rugged service.

> **SAMUEL ELIOT MORISON**

We are tied to the ocean. And when we go back to the sea, whether . . .
it is to sail or to watch it, we are going back from whence we came.

> **PRESIDENT JOHN F. KENNEDY**, 1962. Kennedy served in the U.S. Navy in
> the South Pacific during WWII and was an avid sailor.

The sea is the mother-death and she is a mighty female, the one who
wins, the one who sucks us all up.

> **ANNE SEXTON** from 'A Small Journey' in *The Poet's Story*, 1971

I returned to the sea of necessity, because it would support a boat.

> **E. B. WHITE** from 'The Sea and the Wind that Blows', 1977

When does a man quit the sea? How dizzy, how bumbling must he be?
Does he quit while he's ahead, or wait till he makes some major mistake, like falling overboard or being flattened by an accidental jibe?

> **E. B. WHITE** from 'The Sea and the Wind that Blows', 1977

The ocean doesn't care about you. It makes your boat feel tiny.

> **TRACY KIDDER** from *The Soul of a New Machine*, 1981

My own attitude towards the sea is basically very practical. I want to go
somewhere; my home and my vehicle is a boat, which sails on the sea
and leads to wherever I want to go.

TRISTAN JONES from *Yarns*, 1983

The wind speaks the message of the sun to the sea, and the sea trans-
mits it on through the waves. The wave is the messenger, the water the
medium.

DREW KAMPION

When people for whom no other wilderness remains dream of a ritual
self-purification in heroic solitude, they dream of what John MacGregor
called 'the wholesome sea'.

JONATHAN RABAN from *Coasting*, 1986

In many ways, the ocean is the great equalizer. Egos diminish in the
face of a 40-knot wind and fifteen-foot waves.

DENNIS CONNER from *Comeback: My Race for the America's Cup*, 1987

Serious bodies of water don't have to be large; they can inspire respect
because of idiosyncratic moods.

HERB PAYSON from the article 'Leaving Is Half the Battle', 1989

The sea gives no guarantees.

STEVE CALLAHAN from the article 'Fastnet', 1989

The sea lies on the far margin of society, and it is—as nothing else is—
serious and deep.

JONATHAN RABAN from *The Oxford Book of the Sea*, 1992

If the sea is sick, we'll feel it. If it dies, we die. Our future and the state
of the oceans are one.

SYLVIA EARLE from *Sea Change*, 1995

The sea is antidote to rude traffic jams, to dirt, to disillusion and tired eyes. It reminds us that somewhere beyond our crowded sidewalks and cramped offices, somewhere out there in the wallowing blue beyond the margin, great things are happening. For some of us, the sea is a necessary dimension of getting away.

> **JENNIFER ACKERMAN** from the essay 'When the Sea Calls', 1997

Something in the water's wide spread both fills the mind and empties it.

> **JENNIFER ACKERMAN** from the essay 'When the Sea Calls', 1997

The ocean has always been a salve to my soul...the best thing for a cut or abrasion was to go swimming in salt water. Later down the road of life, I made the discovery that salt water was also good for the mental abrasions one inevitably acquires on land.

> **JIMMY BUFFETT** from *A Pirate Looks at Fifty*, 1998

Seamanship

It's always easier to shake out a reef than to take one in.

> Nautical saying

Take care of the ship and the ship will take care of you.

> Nautical saying

One hand for the ship, one hand for yourself.

> Nautical saying

To a poor sailor, every wind is against him.

> Nautical saying

Seamanship...is a matter of art, and will not admit of being taken up occasionally as an occupation for times of leisure; on the contrary, it is so exacting as to leave leisure for nothing else.

> **PERICLES** as quoted by Thucydides in *The Peloponnesian War*. Pericles is speaking to the Athenian assembly, ca. 431 BC.

A great pilot can sail even when his canvas is rent.

> **SENECA** from 'Epistles'

The pilot...who has been able to say 'Neptune, you shall never sink this ship except on an even keel,' has fulfilled the requirements of his art.

> **SENECA** from 'Epistles'

Item, if any Mariner or officer inferiour shal be found by his labour not meete nor worthie the place that he is presently shipped for, such person may bee unshipped and put on lande at any place within the kings Majesties realme & dominion, and one other person more able and worthy to be put in his place, at the discretion of the captaine and masters...

> **SEBASTIAN CABOT**'s Ordinances of 1553

Ships are to little purpose without skillful Sea Men.

> **RICHARD HAKLUYT** from *Voyages*, 1589

When I call to mind, how many noble ships have been lost, how many worthy persons have been drenched in the sea, and how greatly this Realm has been impoverished by loss of great Ordinance and other rich commodities through the ignorance of our Sea-men, I have greatly wished there were a Lecture of Navigation read in this City, for the banishing of our former gross ignorance in Marine causes, and for the increase and general multiplying of the sea-knowledge in this age...

> **RICHARD HAKLUYT** from *Principal Navigations*, Volume I, 1598. Hakluyt is urging the establishment of a school of navigation in London.

The mistaking of a rope, by an unskilful person, either in a fight or upon a lee shore, may be the loss of all.

Reasons Against the Proposition of Lessening the Number of Men Aboard the King's Ships, ca. 1619

Have a care therefore when there is more sail than ballast.

WILLIAM PENN from 'Some Fruits of Solitude', 1693

As I saw them all busy doing something, I asked Col, with much earnestness, what I could do. He, with a happy readiness, put into my hand a rope, which was fixed to the top of one of the masts, and told me to hold it till he bade me pull. If I had considered the matter, I might have seen that this could not be of the least service; but his object was to keep me out of the way of those who were busy working the vessel, and at the same time to divert my fear, by employing me, and making me think that I was of use. Thus did I stand firm to my post, while the wind and the rain beat upon me, always expecting a call to pull my rope.

JAMES BOSWELL from *Journal of a Tour to the Hebrides*, 1785

Watchfulness is the law of the ship,—watch on watch, for advantage and for life.

RALPH WALDO EMERSON from *English Traits*, 1865

Men often ask when it is time to reef. It is always time to reef when you think it is. The moment you would feel easier and your boat handles better by having less sail spread is the time to shorten down.

THOMAS FLEMING DAY

Seamanship is an entirely different matter. It is not learned in a day, nor in many days; it requires years.

JACK LONDON from *The Cruise of the Snark*, 1911

If you cannot handle your craft by yourself, you ought not to go.

ALAN VILLIERS, 1938

A knot is never 'nearly right'; it is either exactly right or it is hopelessly wrong, one or the other; there is nothing in between.

CLIFFORD ASHLEY from *The Ashley Book of Knots*

Literacy has helped seamanship very little.

SAMUEL ELIOT MORISON

Those who loll around and dream while on watch only show their ignorance of the sea.

L. FRANCIS HERRESHOFF, ca. 1950

Keep out of trouble. It is a disgrace to call for help when you have gotten yourself into trouble through ignorance and carelessness. Father Neptune has no patience with those who do not respect him.

L. FRANCIS HERRESHOFF, ca. 1950

A good seaman, when he boards another vessel, has his eyes everywhere but on the comfort—or lack of it—below, or on the gadgets and fancy gear. He is watching the rigging, the deck fittings, the way the gear is stowed, the way the wires are spliced, and the way lines are coiled. Whatever he does, he is always learning.

TRISTAN JONES from *Yarns*, 1983

It's scary to have a 30-foot wave chasing you. If you're steering, you don't look back. The crew looks back for you, and you watch their faces. When they look straight up, get ready.

MAGNUS OLSSON, helmsman of *EF Language* during Leg Two of the 1997–1998 Whitbread Around the World Race, 1998

Seasickness

Rush to the rail. Hope not for a charitable hand to hold thy head, for all near split themselves with laughter.

Medieval bishop

Bestow the boat, boat-swain, anon,
That our pylgrymms may play thereon;
For some are like to cough and groan
   Ere it be full midnight.
Haul the bowline! Now veer the sheet!
Cook, make ready anon our meat!
Our pylgrymms have no lust to eat:
   I pray God give them rest.
Thys meane'whyle the pylgrymms lie,
And have their bowls all fast them by,
And cry after hot malvesy—
   'Their health to restore'.

>15th century English sea song. These verses are from the oldest known
>authentic English sea song. They refer to seasickness among passengers on a
>merchant ship. Malvesy was a strong, sweet wine.

A boisterous sea will make a man not bred on it so sick, that it bereaves
him of legs and stomach and courage, so much as to fight with his
meat.

SIR WILLIAM MONSON from *Naval Tracts*, 1682

I kept above, that I might have fresh air, and finding myself not affected
by the motion of the vessel, I exulted in being a stout seaman, while Dr
Johnson was in quite a state of annihilation. But I was soon humbled;
for after imagining that I could go with ease to America or the East-
Indies, I became very sick, but kept above board, though it rained hard.

JAMES BOSWELL from *Journal of a Tour to the Hebrides*, 1785

If a person suffer much from seasickness, let him weigh it heavily in the
balance. I speak from experience; it is no trifling evil, cured in a week.

CHARLES DARWIN

Our passengers now made their appearance, and I had for the first time
the opportunity of seeing what a miserable and forlorn creature a sea-
sick passenger is... I will own there was a pleasant feeling of superiority
in being able to walk the deck, and eat, and go about, and comparing
one's self with two poor, miserable, pale creatures staggering and

shuffling about decks... A well man at sea has little sympathy with one who is seasick...

RICHARD HENRY DANA from *Two Years Before the Mast*, 1840

As sick as a lady passenger.

Sailor's expression

I read in bed (but to this hour I don't know what) a good deal; and reeled on deck a little; drank cold brandy-and-water with an unspeakable disgust, and ate hard biscuit perseveringly; not ill, but going to be.

CHARLES DICKENS from *American Notes*, 1842

We all like to see people sea-sick when we are not ourselves.

MARK TWAIN from *The Innocents Abroad*, 1869

Nothing annoys me more than to find that, after having sailed tens and tens and thousands of miles, I cannot cure myself of sea-sickness...many are the days when nothing but the firmest determination not to think about it, but to find something to do, and to do it with all my might keeps me on my feet at all. Fewer, happily, are the days when struggling is of no avail, when I am utterly and hopelessly incapacitated...and when no effort of will can enable me to do what I most wish to accomplish.

LADY ANNA BRASSEY from *A Voyage in the Sunbeam*, 1881. Mrs. Brassey circumnavigated on her husband's luxury yacht *Sunbeam* in 1876 and 1877; she traveled with her husband, children, servants, and a large crew.

The rigging, the sails, the anchors, the cables, the boats, the decks, all have their separate interest; every puff of wind, every catspaw, is a source of entertainment, and when the breeze comes, and, with everything drawing below and aloft, you tear along ten or twelve knots an hour, the sensation of pleasure is complete—if you are not sick.

SIR EDWARD SULLIVAN

I wanted only two things: to feel well again, and to be back on terra firma. Neither seemed likely.

TOM WICKER from 'Rough Passage', 1988

If you get seasick, don't expect a lot of sympathy or attention. Do you what you need to do to leeward; other than that, be as useful as you can, given your condition.

JANICE MOHLHENRICH from the article 'If Only Someone Would Ask Me', 1997

Shipbuilding

On the fifth day I drew its plan.
One acre was its whole floorspace; ten dozen cubits the height
    of each wall;
ten dozen cubits its deck, square on each side.
I laid out the contours, drew it all.
I gave it six decks
and divided it, thus, into seven parts.
Its innards I divided into nine parts.
I struck water-plugs into it.
I checked the poles and laid in all that was necessary.
[For the hull] I poured 24,000 gallons of bitumen into the kiln;
the same amount I laid on the inside.

From *Gilgamesh,* a Sumerian epic poem, ca. 2700 BC. Translated from the Sin-leqi-unninni version by John Gardner and John Maier, 1984.

Twenty trees in all he felled, and then trimmed them with the axe of bronze, and deftly smoothed them, and over them made straight the line. Meanwhile Calypso, the fair goddess, brought him augers, so he bored each piece and jointed them together, and then made all fast with treenails and dowels. Wide as is the floor of a broad ship of burden, which some man well skilled in carpentry may trace him out, of such beam did Odysseus fashion his broad raft. And thereat he wrought, and set up the deckings, fitting them to the close-set uprights, and finished them off with long gunwales, and there he set a mast, and a yard arm

fitted thereto, and moreover he made him a rudder to guide the craft...
Meanwhile Calypso, the fair goddess, brought him web of cloth to
make him sails; and these too he fashioned very skillfully. And he made
fast therein braces and halyards and sheets, and at last he pushed the
raft with levers down to the fair salt sea.

> **HOMER** from *The Odyssey*, ca. 700 BC. The poet describes Odysseus
> constructing his ship.

They made all your planks
  of fir trees from Senir;
they took a cedar from Lebanon
  to make a mast for you.
Of oaks of Bashan
  they made your oars;
they made your decks of pines
  from the coasts of Cyprus,
  inlaid with ivory.
  Of fine embroidered linen from Egypt
  was your sail,
  serving as your ensign;
blue and purple from the coasts of
Elishah
  was your awning.
The inhabitants of Sidon and
  Arvad
  were your rowers;
skilled men of Zemer were in you,
  they were your pilots.
The elders of Gebal and her skilled
  men were in you,
  caulking your seams...

> The Holy Bible, Revised Standard Version, Ezekiel 27:5-9

They filled with light hay the skins from their tents, and drew them
together and stitched them so that the water could not come in.

> **XENOPHON** describing the way in which Cyrus' army constructed boats to
> cross the Euphrates River, ca. 375 BC

...for the materials, collected timber from Mount Etna...then, partly from Italy and partly from Sicily, the wood for treenails and pegs, the upper and lower parts of the frames, and other elements; for cordage, esparto from Spain and hemp and pitch from the Rhone valley; and the rest of his needs from a variety of places. He recruited carpenters and other craftsmen, chose one of them, Archias of Corinth, to be foreman, pressed him to set right to work, and gave the project his personal attention daily.

> **ATHENAEUS** describing the construction of a freighter built for Hiero II, King of Syracuse, in Sicily, ca. 230 BC. Translation by Lionel Casson.

But to be excellent in this faculty is the master-peece of all the most necessary workmen in the world. The first rule of modell thereof being directed by God himselfe to Noah for his Arke, which he never did to any other building but his Temple...

> **CAPTAIN JOHN SMITH** from *Advertisements*, 1631

Build me straight, O worthy Master!
Staunch and strong, a goodly vessel,
That shall laugh at all disaster,
And with wave and whirlwind wrestle!

> **HENRY WADSWORTH LONGFELLOW** from the poem 'The Building of the Ship', 1849

She starts,—she moves,—she seems to feel
The thrill of life along her keel.

> **HENRY WADSWORTH LONGFELLOW** from the poem 'The Building of the Ship', 1849

Boatbuilders are often very conservative, because they have to deal with the safety of the men who go in the boats.

> **T. C. LETHBRIDGE** from *Boats and Boatmen*, 1952

It takes the knowledge of many crafts to make a master boatbuilder. If you can design and build a wooden boat, you can make anything.

> **ROBERT PROTHERO**, founder of the Northwest School of Wooden Boatbuilding in Port Townsend, Washington, 1984

If you've worked on the building of a boat, it belongs to you for the rest of your life.

ROBERT PROTHERO, 1988

...this was good news, that something like a boat could be so much of a construction, all according to the rules of the sea, and that there was a means of making your tenuous way across this world that clearly reflected a long history of thought.

E. L. DOCTOROW from *Billy Bathgate*, 1989

Shiphandling

Anyone can hold the helm when the sea is calm.

PUBLILIUS SYRUS, 1st century BC

Haul the bowline! Now veer the sheet!
Yo ho! Furl'em! Haul in the brails!
Oh, see how well our good ship sails.

GEOFFREY CHAUCER, 1378

Heigh, my hearts! Cheerly, cheerly, my hearts! Yare, yare! Take in the topsail! Tend to th' Master's whistle! Blow, till thou burst thy wind, if room enough!

WILLIAM SHAKESPEARE from *The Tempest*, 1611. Boatswain's speech, act I, scene I.

In a calm sea every man is a pilot.

JOHN RAY from *English Proverbs*, 1670

Handling one's ship in narrow waters, preferably where one has never been before, is the finest sport in the world.

R. D. GRAHAM

It takes several years for anyone to learn to handle a yacht reasonably well, and a lifetime to admit how much more there is to learn.

MAURICE GRIFFITHS

If...you feel, when laying your hand upon the rail, that you are in contact with something alive, responsive to your slightest touch, something that is part of you, something that you really love, then you are in a good position to become truly expert at shiphandling—if you have the knack and are gifted with good judgment and have an eye for distance and are the calm rather than the excitable type.

CAPTAIN H. A. V. VON PFLUGK from *Merchant Marine Officers' Handbook Tips on Practical Shiphandling*

Ships

Praise a slim ship, but put your goods in a fat one.

HESIOD from *The Works and the Days*, ca. 700 BC

Of seas, ships are the grace.

Greek hymn, 5th century BC

The season of ships is here,
The west wind and the swallows;
Flowers in the fields appear,
And the ocean of hills and hollows
Has calmed its waves and is clear.
Free that anchor and chain!
Set your full canvas flying,
O men in the harbor lane:
It is I, Priapus, crying.
Sail out on your trades again!

LEONIDAS OF TARENTUM, 3rd century BC. Translated by Clive Sansom.

Who wishes to give himself an abundance of trouble, let him equip...a ship and a woman...for neither is ever sufficiently adorned.

>PLAUTUS, ca. 200 BC

What a size the ship was! One hundred and eighty feet in length, the ship's carpenter told me, the beam more than a quarter of that, and forty-four feet from the deck to the bottom, the deepest point in the bilge. What a mast it had, what a yard it carried, what a forestay it held up! The way the sternpost rose in a gradual curve with a gilded goose-head set on the tip of it, matched at the opposite end by the forward, more flattened, rise of the prow with the figure of Isis, the goddess the ship was named after, on each side! And the rest of the decoration, the paintings, the red pennant on the main yard, the anchors and the capstan and winches on the foredeck, the accommodations toward the stern—it all seemed like marvels to me! The crew must have been as big as an army. They told me she carried so much grain that it would be enough to feed every mouth in Athens for a year.

>LUCIAN from *Navigium*. He is describing a grain carrier which worked the Alexandria to Rome route when it unexpectedly called in Athens, ca. 250 AD. Translation by Lionel Casson.

...a dull sailer and unfit for discovery.

>CHRISTOPHER COLUMBUS' description of *Santa Maria*

A rotten carcass of a boat, not rigg'd,
Nor tackle, sail, nor mast; the very rats
Instinctively have quit it.

>WILLIAM SHAKESPEARE from *The Tempest*, 1611. Speech of Prospero, act I, scene II.

Of all fabricks a ship is the most excellent, requiring more art in building, rigging, sayling, trimming, defending, and moaring...

>CAPTAIN JOHN SMITH from *Advertisements*, 1631

I wish to have no Connection with any Ship that does not sail fast, for I intend to go in harm's way.

>JOHN PAUL JONES, 1778

...a ship is like a lady's watch, always out of repair.

RICHARD HENRY DANA from *Two Years Before the Mast*, 1840

Notwithstanding all that has been said about the beauty of a ship under full sail, there are very few who have ever seen a ship, literally, under all her sail. A ship coming in or going out of port, with her ordinary sails, and perhaps two or three studding-sails, is commonly said to be under full sail; but a ship never has all her sail upon her, except when she has a light, steady breeze, very nearly, but not quite dead aft, and so regular that it can be trusted, and is likely to last for some time. Then, with all her sails, light and heavy, and studding-sails, on each side, alow and aloft, she is the most glorious moving object in the world. Such a sight, very few, even some who have been at sea a great deal, have ever beheld; for from the deck of your own vessel you cannot see her, as you would a separate object.

RICHARD HENRY DANA from *Two Years Before the Mast*, 1840

Give me a big ship. There is more room, more hands, better outfit, better regulation, more life, and more company.

RICHARD HENRY DANA from *Two Years Before the Mast*, 1840

I crept below at midnight. It was not exactly comfortable below. It was decidedly close; and it was impossible to be unconscious of the presence of that extraordinary compound of strange smells, which is to be found nowhere but onboard ship, and which is such a subtle perfume that it seems to enter at every pore of the skin, and whisper of the hold.

CHARLES DICKENS from *American Notes*, 1842. Dickens made a transatlantic crossing in the 1840s.

It is impossible not to personify a ship; everybody does, in everything they say—she behaves well; she minds her rudder; she swims like a duck; she runs her nose into the water; she looks into a port. Then that wonderful *esprit de corps*, by which we adopt into our self-love everything we touch, makes us all champions of her sailing qualities.

RALPH WALDO EMERSON from *English Traits*, 1865

Take it all in all, a ship is the most honourable thing that man, as a gregarious animal, has ever produced.

JOHN RUSKIN

...the ship, a fragment detached from the earth, went on lonely and swift like a small planet. Round her the abysses of sky and sea met in an unattainable frontier. A great circular solitude moved with her, ever changing and ever the same, always monotonous and always imposing.

JOSEPH CONRAD from *The Nigger of the Narcissus*, 1897

She wants some repairs.

JOSHUA SLOCUM from *Sailing Alone Around the World*, 1900, quoting Captain Eben Pierce who gave him *Spray* after the vessel had sat untended in a field for seven years. Slocum essentially rebuilt the vessel.

Porpoises always prefer sailing ships.

JOSHUA SLOCUM from *Sailing Alone Around the World*, 1900

Even while the storm raged at its worst, my ship was wholesome and noble. My mind as to her seaworthiness was put at ease for aye.

JOSHUA SLOCUM, from *Sailing Alone Around the World*, 1900. Slocum is describing his sloop *Spray* during a storm while rounding Cape Horn.

The love that is given to ships is profoundly different from the love men feel for every other work of their hands.

JOSEPH CONRAD from *The Mirror of the Sea*, 1906

A ship in a dock, surrounded by quays and the walls of warehouses, has the appearance of a prisoner meditating upon freedom in the sadness of a free spirit put under restraint.

JOSEPH CONRAD from *The Mirror of the Sea*, 1906

...a new ship receives as much attention as if she were a young bride.

JOSEPH CONRAD from *The Mirror of the Sea*, 1906

For that the worst of ships would repent if she were ever given time I make no doubt. I have known too many of them. No ship is wholly bad.

JOSEPH CONRAD from *The Mirror of the Sea*, 1906

Did not Emerson say that every ship seems romantic, except that on which we sail?

WILLARD L. SPERRY

Never in these United States has the brain of man conceived, or the hand of man fashioned, so perfect a thing as the clipper ship. In her, the long-suppressed artistic impulse of a practical, hard-worked race burst into flower...for a brief moment of time they flashed their splendor around the world, then disappeared...

SAMUEL ELIOT MORISON from *The Maritime History of Massachusetts*, 1921

Unless a man feels that his ship can encounter a heavy gale with success, he cannot put to sea in her with any confidence; and there is nothing which gives him so great a feeling of pride and security in her as the experience of such a gale encountered without mishap.

EVELYN GEORGE MARTIN, 1928

A ship is always referred to as 'she' because it costs so much to keep her in paint and powder.

ADMIRAL CHESTER W. NIMITZ, 1940

She gathered way, then crash! she struck an onrushing sea that swept her fore and aft even to the mastheads. While all baled and pumped for dear life, she seemed to stop, then again charged a galloping wall of water, slam! like striking a stone wall with such force that the bow planks opened and lines of water spurted in from every seam, as she halted, trembling, and then leaped forward again. The strains, shocks, and blows were tremendous, threatening every minute to start her planking, while the bow seams opened and closed on every sea. Good boat! but how she stood it was a miracle of God's mercy.

F. A. WORSLEY from *Shackleton's Boat Journey* describing a storm off the Antarctic coast, 1940

Boats, automobiles, and liquor all have their thrills, but either they do not last long or they cost a lot to keep up.

L. FRANCIS HERRESHOFF, ca. 1950

I think it is interesting that we have come back to star- and space *ships*. *Jet* will do for a transport shorthand; yet when man really reaches, across the vast seas of space, he still reaches in ships.

JOHN FOWLES from *Shipwreck*, 1974

Shipwreck

...we were caught by a terrific squall from the west that snapped the forestays of the mast so that it fell aft, while all the ship's gear tumbled about at the bottom of the vessel. The mast fell upon the head of the helmsman in the ship's stern... Then Zeus let fly with his thunderbolts, and the ship went round and round, and was filled with fire and brimstone as the lightning struck it. The men all fell into the sea... I stuck to the ship till the sea knocked her sides from her keel (which drifted about by itself) and struck the mast out of her in the direction of the keel; but there was a backstay of stout ox-thong still hanging about, and with this I lashed the mast and keel together, and getting astride of them was carried wherever the winds chose to take me.

HOMER from *The Odyssey*, ca. 700 BC

Three times I have been shipwrecked; a night and a day I have been adrift at sea.

The Holy Bible, Revised Standard Version, II Corinthians 11:25

Now when it was day, they did not recognize the land, but they noticed a bay with a beach, on which they planned if possible to bring the ship ashore. So they cast off the anchors and left them in the sea, at the same time loosening the ropes that tied the rudders; then hoisting the foresail to the wind they made for the beach. But striking a shoal they ran the vessel aground; the bow stuck and remained immovable, and the stern was broken up by the surf.

The Holy Bible, Revised Standard Version, Acts 27:39–41

...the wind rose, and blew vehemently at South by East, bringing withal raine, and thicke mist, so that we could not see a cable length before us. And betimes in the morning we were altogether runne and folded in amongst flats and sands, amongst which we found shoale and deepe in every three or foure shippes length, after we began to sound...the *Delight*...was yet foremost upon the breach, keeping so ill watch, that they knew not the danger, before they felt the same, too late to recover it: for presently the Admiral struck ground, and had soone after her stern and hinder parts beaten in pieces...we desired to save the men by every possible meanes. But all in vaine, sith God had determined their ruine.

> **CAPTAIN EDWARD HAYES** describing the loss of the *Delight* in August 1583 off Sable Island, Nova Scotia, during Sir Humphrey Gilbert's second and final voyage to America

...Monday night, about twelve of the clocke, or not long after, the Frigat being ahead of us in the *Golden Hinde,* suddenly her lights went out, whereof as it were in a moment, we lost the sight, and withall our watch cryed, the General was cast away, which was too true. For on that moment the Frigat was devoured and swallowed up of the Sea...

> **CAPTAIN EDWARD HAYES'** description of the loss of the pinnace *Squirrel* and the death of Sir Humphrey Gilbert in the Atlantic on September 9, 1583

He, who has suffer'd Ship-wrack, feares to saile
Upon the Seas, though with a gentle gale.

> **ROBERT HERRICK** from 'Hesperides' (Ship-wrack), 1648

I was surprised to see, in all the way from Winterton, that the farmers, and country people had scarce a barn, or a shed, or a stable; nay, not the pales of their yards, and garden, not a hogsty, not a necessary-house, but what was built of old planks, beams, wales and timbers, &c. the wrecks of ships, and ruins of mariners' and merchants' fortunes.

> **DANIEL DEFOE** from *A Tour through the Whole Island of Great Britain*. He is describing the British coast around Yarmouth on a trip he took in 1724–1726.

I found that it would not do to speak of shipwrecks there, for almost every family has lost some of its members at sea. 'Who lives in that house?' I inquired. 'Three widows' was the reply.

> **HENRY DAVID THOREAU** from *Cape Cod*, 1865. He refers to the town of Dennis on Cape Cod.

There are more consequences to a shipwreck than the underwriters notice.

> **HENRY DAVID THOREAU** from *Cape Cod*, 1865

The annals of this voracious beach! Who could write them, unless it were a shipwrecked sailor? How many who have seen it have seen it only in the midst of danger and distress, the last strip of earth which their mortal eyes beheld.

> **HENRY DAVID THOREAU** from *Cape Cod*, 1865

When a real nor'easter blows, howling landward through the winter night over a thousand miles of gray, tormented seas, all shipping off the Cape must pass the Cape or strand. In the darkness and scream of the storm, in the beat of the endless, icy, crystalline snow, rigging freezes, sails freeze and tear—of a sudden the long booming undertone of the surf sounds under the lee bow—a moment's drift, the feel of surf twisting the keel of the vessel, then a jarring, thundering crash and the upward drive of the bar.

> **HENRY BESTON** from *The Outermost House*, 1928. He describes a shipwreck on Cape Cod.

As we looked at that hellish rock-bound coast, with its roaring breakers, we wondered, impersonally, at which spot our end was to come.

> **F. A. WORSLEY** from *Shackleton's Boat Journey* describing a storm off the Antarctic coast, 1940

Singlehanding

...I sat and read my books, mended my clothes, or cooked my meals and ate them in peace. I had already found that it was not good to be alone, and so I made companionship with what there was around me, sometimes with the universe and sometimes with my own insignificant self; but my books were always my friends, let fail all else. Nothing could be easier or more restful than my voyage in the trade-winds.

    JOSHUA SLOCUM from *Sailing Alone Around the World*, 1900

The acute pain of solitude experienced at first never returned. I had penetrated a mystery... I had met Neptune in his wrath, but he found that I had not treated him with contempt, and so he suffered me to go on and explore.

    JOSHUA SLOCUM from *Sailing Alone Around the World*, 1900

One must make a long sea voyage to realize the immensity and solitude of the sea.

    JEAN GAU, French singlehander and circumnavigator

It isn't that life ashore is distasteful to me. But life at sea is better.

    TOM DRAKE, small boat and singlehanded sailor. He disappeared in the Pacific in 1936.

There are a lot of people who think that a man who sails alone stops at night.

    MARIN-MARIE from *Wind Aloft, Wind Alow*, 1947

I began to feel the loneliness less acutely as my goal approached, though at the same time I hated the thought of arriving.

    MARIN-MARIE from *Wind Aloft, Wind Alow*, 1947

The best way to find peace is to sail alone.

    MARIN-MARIE

The first night...is the loneliest of the passage. I have found when singlehanded that the longer I am at sea the less I feel the loneliness and the more company I find in the sky, the wind, the waves, my boat and even in myself.

BILL HOWELL

Much of the joy of solitude comes from making some contact with one's inner being. In stripping away the jumble of distractions, or society's expectations, or the professional mask (persona), the individual makes contact with something which is uniquely himself. This does not have to lead on to lofty states of awareness, simply to a profound sense of tranquillity and sense of meaningfulness.

SIR FRANCIS CHICHESTER, 1967

When I am alone on an adventure I become more efficient and become vitalized... It seems to me that all one's sensations are magnified, the sensation of excitement, the feeling of accomplishment, fear, perhaps, and of pleasure. All one's senses are more acute. One becomes so tuned up that the slightest change of conditions, of weather, of noise, or movement will be perceived and, in fact, will wake one up after being alone for a while. Another curious thing about solitude is that time seems to change its rate. Sometimes there seems to be a long interval between two words you are thinking, as if you dropped them separately into a pool.

SIR FRANCIS CHICHESTER

At sea, I learned how little a person needs, not how much.

ROBIN LEE GRAHAM

I liked to sail alone. The sea was the same as a girl to me—I did not want anyone else along.

E. B. WHITE from 'The Sea and the Wind that Blows', 1977

In attempting this voyage I risked losing a life that had at last become fulfilling; but in carrying it out I experienced a second life, a life so separate and complete it appeared to have little relation to the old one that went before.

> **NAOMI JAMES** from *Alone Around the World*. She is describing the conclusion of her solo circumnavigation, June 1978.

Sinking

We were not much more than a quarter of an hour out of our ship but we saw her sink, and then I understood for the first time what was meant by a ship foundering in the sea…

> **DANIEL DEFOE** from *Robinson Crusoe*, 1719

A ship which is about to sink makes her lamentations just like any other human being.

> **JAMES FENIMORE COOPER** from *The Red Rover*, 1828

Get clear of the ship fast! Stay together. God bless you.

> Final words of **CAPTAIN DIEBITSCH** to the crew of the four-masted steel barque *Pamir* during Hurricane Carrie in September 1957. The ship sank in the Atlantic, and all but 6 of the 86 crew and cadets onboard perished.

I had fleeting glimpses of her hull above the jagged silhouette of the waves, then all I could see was her riding light waving bravely amongst the tumult. As I watched, the sea reached her batteries, the light grew suddenly bright, flickered and went out.

> **NIGEL TETLEY** from *Trimaran Solo*, 1970. His trimaran *Victress* sank during a round-the-world race in 1969.

Sounds

...it is a mistake to talk of the monotone of ocean or of the monotonous nature of its sound. The sea has many voices. Listen to its surf, really lend it your ears, and you will hear in it a world of sounds: hollow boomings and heavy roarings, great watery tumblings and tramplings, long hissing seethes, sharp, rifle-shot reports, splashes, whispers, the grinding undertone of stones, and sometimes vocal sounds that might be the half-heard talk of people in the sea.

HENRY BESTON from *The Outermost House*, 1928

Every mood of the wind, every change in the day's weather, every phase of the tide—all these have subtle sea musics all their own.

HENRY BESTON from *The Outermost House*, 1928

The three great elemental sounds in nature are the sound of rain, the sound of wind in a primeval wood, and the sound of outer ocean on a beach. I have heard them all, and of the three elemental voices, that of ocean is the most awesome, beautiful, and varied.

HENRY BESTON from *The Outermost House*, 1928

The sound of the sea is the most time-effacing sound there is. The centuries reroll in a cloud and the earth becomes green again when you listen, with eyes shut, to the sea.

E. B. WHITE from 'On a Florida Key', 1941

If you consider the hull as a ship's body and the sails her means of locomotion, the 'lines', as seamen called the ropes, were her nerves and tendons. The wind blowing on this intricate network of cordage made a deep humming noise in a fresh gale and a high-pitched whistle in a storm; halyards slatting against the spars provided the woodwind; the sails spilling wind and then filling out with a hollow boom were the percussion instruments; and the rush of great waters the organ accompaniment—in a symphony of sound that was music to a seaman's ear.

SAMUEL ELIOT MORISON from *The Ropemakers of Plymouth*, 1950

Stars

Next to seeing land, there is no sight which makes one realize more that
he is drawing near home, than to see the same heavens, under which he
was born, shining at night over his head.

> **RICHARD HENRY DANA** from *Two Years Before the Mast*, 1840. Dana is
> writing about his return onboard the *Alert* from California to Boston.

...sailors say that in coming home from round Cape Horn, and the Cape
of Good Hope, the north star is the first land you make.

> **RICHARD HENRY DANA** from *Two Years Before the Mast*, 1840

In the luminous east, two great stars aslant were rising clear of the
exhalations of darkness gathered at the rim of night and ocean—
Betelgeuse and Bellatrix, the shoulders of Orion. Autumn had come,
and the Giant stood again at the horizon of day and the ebbing year, his
belt still hidden in the bank of cloud, his feet in the deeps of space and
the far surges of the sea.

> **HENRY BESTON** from *The Outermost House*, 1928

Storms

Save the ship if you'd save yourself.

> Sailor's adage

Sailors have a port in every storm.

> Sailor's proverb

It takes a good storm to get the best out of a good sailor.

> Nautical saying

Six days and seven nights
the wind shrieked, the stormflood rolled through the land.
On the seventh day of its coming the stormflood broke from the
battle which had labored like a woman giving birth.
The sea grew quiet, the storm was still...

> From *Gilgamesh*, a Sumerian epic poem, ca. 2700 BC. Translated from the Sin-leqi-unninni version by John Gardner and John Maier, 1984.

Then they cried to the Lord in their trouble,
and he delivered them from their distress;
he made the storm be still,
and the waves of the sea were hushed.

> The Holy Bible, Revised Standard Version, Psalms 107:28–29

Now Zeus, gatherer of the clouds, aroused the North Wind against our
ships with a terrible tempest, and covered land and sea alike with
clouds, and down sped night from heaven. Thus the ships were driven
headlong, and their sails were torn to shreds by the might of the wind.
So we lowered the sails into the hold, in fear of death, but rowed the
ships landward apace. There for two nights and two days we lay
continually, consuming our hearts with weariness and sorrow.

> **HOMER** from *The Odyssey*, ca. 700 BC

...the great wave smote down upon him, driving on in terrible wise,
that the raft heeled again. And far therefrom he fell, and lost the helm
from his hand; and the fierce blast of the jostling winds came and brake
his mast in the midst, and sail and yard-arm fell afar into the deep.

> **HOMER** from *The Odyssey*, ca. 700 BC

We spread our sails before the willing wind.
Now from the sight of land our galleys move,
With only seas around and skies above;
When o'er our heads descends a burst of rain,
And night with sable clouds involves the main;
The ruffling winds the foamy billows raise;
The scatter'd fleet is forc'd to sev'ral ways;
The face of heav'n is ravish'd from our eyes,

And in redoubled peals the roaring thunder flies.
Cast from our course, we wander in the dark.
No stars to guide, no point of land to mark.

> **VIRGIL** from the *Aeneid*, Book III

The men groaned, the women shrieked, everybody called upon God,
cried aloud, remembered their dear ones. Only Amarantus was in good
spirits, thinking he was going to get out of paying his creditors...

> **SYNESIUS** from *Epistolae*. He describes the worst part of a storm during a
> voyage in the Mediterranean from Alexandria to Cyrene in 404 AD. Translation
> by Lionel Casson.

Blood and wounds! I take God to witness, never hath there been a
tempest so violent since Noah's flood.

> **SIR FRANCIS DRAKE**, commenting on a September storm in 1578 that his
> vessel *Golden Hind* weathered in the Pacific

What though the mast be now blown overboard,
The cable broke, the holding anchor lost,
And half our sailors swallow'd in the flood;
Yet lives our pilot still.

> **WILLIAM SHAKESPEARE** from *The Third Part of King Henry the Sixth*, 1592.
> Speech of Queen Margaret, act V, scene IV.

Then like two mighty Kings, which dwelling farre
Asunder, meet against a third to warre,
The South and West winds joyn'd, and, as they blew,
Waves like a rowling trench before them threw.
Sooner than you read this line, did the gale,
Like shot, not fear'd till felt, our sailes assaile.

> **JOHN DONNE** from 'The Storme', 1633

...it rain'd more than if the Sunne had drunke the sea...

> **JOHN DONNE** from 'The Storme', 1633

...all our tacklings Snapping, like too-high-stretched treble strings...

JOHN DONNE from 'The Storme', 1633

...of all objects that I have ever seen, there is none which affects my imagination so much as the sea or ocean. I cannot see the heaving of this prodigious bulk of waters, even in a calm, without a very pleasing astonishment; but when it is worked up in a tempest, so that the Horizon on every side is nothing but foaming billows and floating mountains, it is impossible to describe the agreeable horror that rises from such a prospect. A troubled ocean, to a man who sails upon it, is, I think, the biggest object he can see in motion, and consequently gives his imagination one of the highest kinds of pleasure that can arise from greatness.

JOSEPH ADDISON from the *Spectator*, 1712

...the storm increas'd, and the sea, which I had never been upon before, went very high... I expected every wave would have swallowed us up, and that every time the ship fell down, as I thought, in the trough or hollow of the sea, we should never rise more; and in this agony of mind I made many vows and resolutions, that if it would please God here to spare my life this one voyage, if I ever got once my foot upon dry land again, I would go directly home to my father, and never set it into a ship again while I lived...

DANIEL DEFOE from *Robinson Crusoe*, 1719

...the storm was so violent, that I saw what is not often seen, the master, the boat-swain, and some others more sensible than the rest, at their prayers, and expecting every moment when the ship would go to the bottom.

DANIEL DEFOE from *Robinson Crusoe*, 1719

A continuation of stormy surprising weather, the elements seeming all confused. In the height of the squall had several violent claps of thunder; before the explosion of which a quick subtle fire ran along our decks which bursting made a report like a pistol and struck several of our men and officers who with the violence of the blow were black and blue in several places. This fire was attended with a strong sulphurous smell.

> **PHILIP SAUMAREZ** of the sloop *Tryal* describing a lightning strike during Anson's circumnavigation, May 1741

...the next morning, endeavouring to hand the top-sails, the clew-lines and bunt-lines broke, and the sheets being half flown, every seam in the top-sails was soon split from top to bottom, and the main top-sail shook so strongly in the wind, that it carried away the top lanthorn, and endangered the head of the mast; however, at length some of the most daring of our men ventured upon the yard, and cut the sail away close to the reefs, though with the utmost hazard to their lives.

> **RICHARD WALTER** from *A Voyage round the World by George Anson*, 1748. Walter is describing the *Centurion*'s passage through the Strait of Le Maire and rounding of Cape Horn in April 1741.

...it was with the end of her bowsprit under water, over which (and the forecastle) these mighty great seas broke in as far aft as the main mast, and as if it had been over a rock; so that we were quite under water, and had not the ship been an extraordinary good sea boat (which was the only good quality she had) she could never have outlived this storm...

> **PHILIP CARTERET**'s description of a storm which his ship *Swallow* weathered near Juan Fernandez Island in the Pacific, ca. 1767

I now saw what I never saw before, a prodigious sea, with immense billows coming upon a vessel, so as that it seemed hardly possible to escape. There was something grandly horrible in the sight. I am glad I have seen it once.

> **JAMES BOSWELL** from a *Journal of a Tour to the Hebrides*, 1785

Any port in a storm.

> **JOHN POOLE** from *Paul Pry*

If you have never been at sea in a heavy gale, you can form no idea of the confusion of mind occasioned by the wind and spray together. They blind, deafen, and strangle you, and take away all power of action or reflection.

> **EDGAR ALLAN POE** from 'A Descent into a Maelstrom', 1845

I have never complained of a heavy sea. On the other hand, I have never praised it for anything but its grandeur, which, in a measure, it was compulsory to behold, whether agreeable or otherwise.

RICHARD T. McMULLEN, early small boat sailor

Heavy weather is when the mode of handling the boat is dictated to you rather than by you.

JOHN RUSSELL of the Royal Yachting Association

It blew day after day: it blew with spite, without interval, without mercy, without rest. The world was nothing but an immensity of great foaming waves rushing at us, under a sky low enough to touch with the hand and dirty like a smoked ceiling. In the stormy space surrounding us there was as much flying spray as air. Day after day and night after night there was nothing round the ship but the howl of the wind, the tumult of the sea, the noise of water pouring over her deck. There was no rest for her and no rest for us. She tossed, she pitched, she stood on her head, she sat on her tail, she rolled, she groaned, and we had to hold on while on deck and cling to our bunks when below, in a constant effort of body and worry of mind.

JOSEPH CONRAD from *Youth*, 1902

If you would know the age of the earth, look upon the sea in a storm.

JOSEPH CONRAD from *The Mirror of the Sea,* 1906

There is infinite variety in the gales of wind at sea, and except for the peculiar, terrible, and mysterious moaning that may be heard some-times passing through the roar of a hurricane—except for that unforget-table sound, as if the soul of the universe had been goaded into a mournful groan—it is, after all, the human voice that stamps the mark of human consciousness upon the character of a gale.

JOSEPH CONRAD from *The Mirror of the Sea,* 1906

The downpours thicken. Preceding each shower a mysterious gloom, like the passage of a shadow above the firmament of grey clouds, filters down upon the ship. Now and then the rain pours upon your head in streams as if from spouts. It seems as if your ship were going to be drowned before she sank, as if all atmosphere had turned to water.

JOSEPH CONRAD from *The Mirror of the Sea*, 1906

Dr. Johnson said that the pleasure of going to sea was getting to shore again; certainly the pleasure of a storm is getting into smooth water again.

SIR EDWARD SULLIVAN

Dante tells us that those who have committed carnal sin are tossed about ceaselessly by the most furious winds in the second circle of Hell. The corresponding hell on earth is found in the southern oceans which encircle the world without break, tempest-tossed by gales which follow one another round and round the world from West to East.

APSLEY CHERRY-GARRARD from *The Worst Journey in the World*, 1922

If the sea shouts an insistent challenge, a sailor can never be truly content until he has voyaged from Fifty South in the Atlantic to Fifty South in the Pacific in his own command. This is the ultimate test, given to very few to know.

WARWICK M. TOMPKINS

That Monday night was as foul and black a night as you could meet at sea. Although it was pitch dark, the white breakers showed in the blackness like monstrous beasts charging down on the yacht. They towered high in the sky, I wouldn't blame anyone for being terrified at the sight. My cross-tree lights showed up the breaking water, white in the black darkness, and now and then a wave caught the hull and breaking against it, sluiced over the decks.

SIR FRANCIS CHICHESTER from *Gipsy Moth Circles the World*. Chichester is describing a storm in the Tasman Sea, January 1967.

With a mighty roar, sounding to our paralyzed ears and frozen minds as if all the wild animals on earth were about to spring on us, *our* sea, the one that had waited for us all these years, after all these thousands of miles, was upon us! I remember thinking to myself, lying spread-

eagled on the cabin deck: *This is it. What a pity I can't see it!* Then, it
seemed, the boat tore asunder.

TRISTAN JONES from *Yarns*, 1983

The time to reef is when you first think about it.

TRISTAN JONES, 1988

Only fools—and racers—track with a storm.

STEVE COLGATE from the article 'The Stages of Heavy-weather Sailing', 1989

Think very hard before you abandon ship into a liferaft. It could be
your last decision.

STEVE COLGATE from the article 'The Stages of Heavy-weather Sailing', 1989

Abovedecks it was a white world. Troughs and monster waves spewed
foam. It was an illogical world run amok, not wicked, but willful; and
yet, at the same time, shockingly indifferent... I noticed my thoughts
had become very land-oriented. Mentally I stroked pastoral images of
meadows and trim English gardens.

KATHRYN LASKY KNIGHT, 1990

T–V

Tides

...tides are the sailor's friend.

SAMUEL ELIOT MORISON from *Spring Tides*, 1964

Voyages

The occasion that moved me to take such a voyage in hand, was only a curiosity of mind, a desire of novelties, and a longing to learn out the bounds of the Ocean.

LUCIAN of Samothrace

He knew the sea, would point the prow
Straight to that distant Danish shore.
Then they sailed, set their ship
Out on the waves, under the cliffs.

Ready for what came they wound through the currents,
The seas beating at the sand, and were borne
In the lap of their shining ship, lined
With gleaming armor, going safely
In that oak-hard boat to where their hearts took
    them.
The wind hurried them over the waves,
The ship foamed through the sea like a bird
Until, in the time they had known it would take,
Standing in the round-curled prow they could see
Sparkling hills, high and green,
Jutting up over the shore, and rejoicing
In those rock-steep cliffs they quietly ended
Their voyage.

> From *Beowulf*, translated by Burton Raffel, 1963. In this 8th century Anglo-Saxon epic poem, the poet describes the voyage of Beowulf and his men from the Land of the Geats to Denmark.

Then the ship left shore, left
    Denmark,
Traveled through deep water. Deck timbers creaked,
And the wind billowing through the sail stretched
From the mast, tied tight with ropes, did not hold
    them
Back, did not keep the ring-prowed ship
From foaming swiftly through the waves, the sea
Currents, across the wide ocean until
They could see familiar headlands, cliffs
That sprang out of Geatish soil.

> From *Beowulf*, translated by Burton Raffel, 1963. In this 8th century Anglo-Saxon epic poem, the poet describes the return of Beowulf and his men from Denmark to the Land of the Geats.

Let me roll around the globe, let me rock upon the sea: let me race and
pant out my life with an eternal breeze and an endless sea before!

HERMAN MELVILLE from *Redburn*, 1849

...under the best of conditions, a voyage is one of the severest tests to try a man.

RALPH WALDO EMERSON from *English Traits*, 1865

To young men contemplating a voyage I would say go... To face the elements is, to be sure, no light matter when the sea is in its grandest mood. You must then know the sea, and know that you know it, and not forget that it was made to be sailed over.

JOSHUA SLOCUM from *Sailing Alone Around the World*, 1900

I must go down to the seas again, to the lonely sea and the sky,
And all I ask is a tall ship and a star to steer her by.

JOHN MASEFIELD from the poem 'Sea Fever', 1902

For how like life is the voyage of the great sailing ship?

ALAN VILLIERS

At sea, every dawn is a thrill.

NICHOLAS MONSARRAT

W–Y

Watch

The watch is changed,
The glass is running.
We shall have a good voyage
If God is willing.

> Medieval sailor's ditty concerning the sand hourglass which measured the
> time a watch section spent on deck.

...the Master being chiefe of the starboord watch doth call one, and his
right hand mate on the larboord doth call one, and so forward till they
be divided in two parts...according to your number and burthen of
your ship...these are to take their turnes at the Helme, trim sailes,
pumpe, and doe all duties...for eight Glasses or four houres...which is a
watch...

> **CAPTAIN JOHN SMITH** from *A Sea Grammar*, 1627. Smith is describing the
> methods of dividing a ship's crew into two watch sections and their duties
> while on watch.

...the following night I stood my first watch. I remained awake nearly all the first part of the night from fear that I might not hear when I was called; and when I went on deck, so great were my ideas of the importance of my trust, that I walked regularly fore and aft the whole length of the vessel, looking out over the bows and taffrail at each turn, and was not a little surprised at the coolness of the old salt whom I called to take my place, in stowing himself snugly away under the long boat, for a nap. That was a sufficient look-out, he thought, for a fine night, at anchor in a safe harbor.

RICHARD HENRY DANA from *Two Years Before the Mast*, 1840

The bells seemed to be an hour or two apart, instead of half an hour, and an age to elapse before the welcome sound of eight bells. The sole object was to make the time pass on.

RICHARD HENRY DANA from *Two Years Before the Mast*, 1840

A crewmember who always shows up 15 minutes early will, curiously enough, rarely worry about relief being 15 minutes late. The crew who always is 15 minutes late will tear the heart out of a relief who has the audacity to take one extra minute. This is an immutable law of the sea.

REESE PALLEY from *There Be No Dragons*, 1996

Water

Those who sleep close to water find tranquillity.

Hawaiian saying

Water is the noblest of the elements.

PINDAR

Under heaven nothing is more soft and yielding than water. Yet for attacking the solid and strong, nothing is better. It has no equal.

LAO-TZU

On land only the grass and trees wave, but the water itself is rippled by the wind.

HENRY DAVID THOREAU from Walden, 1854

Of all inorganic substances...water is the most wonderful.

JOHN RUSKIN

It's funny stuff, water. It washes away your memories and gives you a chance to start afresh. That's why all those religions are so keen to dip you into it.

LEN DEIGHTON

Where from, you growling water? How old are you? Did you come in from the sea with the midnight flood? Were you sired by an iceberg out of the South Polar Cap, or was your dam a cloud knocked up by the High Sierra? Were you falling rain short months ago?

STERLING HAYDEN from *Wanderer*, 1963

Waterspout

There appeared, not far from the mouth of the harbour of St John's, two or three water-spouts, one of which took its course up the harbour. Its progressive motion was slow and unequal, not in a straight line, but as it were by jerks and starts. There appeared in the water a circle of about twenty yards diameter, which to me had a dreadful though pleasing appearance. The water in this circle was violently agitated, being whisked about, and carried up into the air with great rapidity and noise, and reflected a lustre, as if the sun shined bright on that spot, which was more conspicuous, as there appeared a dark circle around it.

WILLIAM FALCONER from *An Universal Dictionary of the Marine*, 1769

They seemed a spectacle, not a danger. To go up in a waterspout would
be an interesting finish, something to break the monotony of being
becalmed.

DORA BIRTLES

Waves

The floods are risen, O Lord
the floods have lifted up their voice:
the floods lift up their waves.
The waves of the sea are mighty,
and rage horribly:
but yet the Lord, who dwelleth on high, is mightier.

Book of Common Prayer, 1662

The bleat, the bark, bellow, and roar
Are waves that beat on Heaven's shore.

WILLIAM BLAKE

I see the waves upon the shore
Like light dissolved in star-showers, thrown.

PERCY BYSSHE SHELLEY from the poem 'Stanzas Written in Dejection, near
Naples'

Once more
upon the waters!
yet once more!
And the waves
bound beneath me
as a steed that
knows his rider.

LORD BYRON from the poem 'Childe Harold's Pilgrimage', 1818

The waves forever rolling to the land are too far-traveling and
untamable to be familiar.

HENRY DAVID THOREAU from *Cape Cod*, 1865

The tossing waves, the foam, the ships in the distance,
The wild unrest, the snowy, curling caps—that inbound urge
and urge of waves,
Seeking the shore forever.

> **WALT WHITMAN** from the poem 'From Montauk Point' in *Leaves of Grass*
> (First Annex: Sands at Seventy), ca. 1889

A singular disadvantage of the sea lies in the fact that after successfully
surmounting one wave you discover that there is another behind it just
as important and just as nervously anxious to do something effective in
the way of swamping boats.

> **STEPHEN CRANE** from *The Open Boat*, 1897

But where, after all, would be the poetry of the sea were there no wild
waves?

> **JOSHUA SLOCUM** from *Sailing Alone Around the World*, 1900

While the sloop was reaching under short sail, a tremendous wave, the
culmination, it seemed, of many waves, rolled down upon her in a
storm, roaring as it came. I had only a moment to get all sail down and
myself upon the peak halyards, out of danger, when I saw the mighty
crest towering masthead-high above me. The mountain of water
submerged my vessel.

> **JOSHUA SLOCUM** from *Sailing Alone Around the World*, 1900

Half a mile out, where is the reef, the whiteheaded combers thrust
suddenly skyward out of the placid turquoise-blue and come rolling in
to shore. One after another they come, a mile long, with smoking crests,
the white battalions of the infinite army of the sea.

> **JACK LONDON** from *The Cruise of the Snark*, 1911. London is describing the
> surf of the Hawaiian islands.

The wind just tore blocks out of the long ridges of the north-westerly
sea, piled Pelion upon Ossa and the resulting pyramid on top of the
huge south-westerly swell that runs without ceasing around the
Southern Ocean, often unnoticed, but rising in an instant at the touch of
its normal wind; and the result was stupendous. I do not suppose it

very often happened that all three sets of waves climbed up on each other's backs, but it happened once within a ship's length of me. Of course the elevation of 40 feet, as I judged it to be, was quite momentary; the pile was entirely top-heavy and the upper 10 feet or so curled over as clean as if it had tripped up on a reef and tumbled all over the ocean.

CONOR O'BRIEN from *Across Three Oceans*, 1927

The rhythm of the waves beats in the sea like a pulse in the living flesh. It is pure force, forever embodying itself in a succession of watery shapes which vanish on its passing.

HENRY BESTON from *The Outermost House*, 1928

The privilege of viewing great storm waves of extreme height is a rare one indeed. Furthermore, we have no assurance that the highest waves of the ocean have been observed or measured. If such a wave should ever be encountered, it is probable that all hands would be chiefly concerned with the safety of the ship to the exclusion of any scientific measurement of the phenomena.

R. P. WHITEMARSH from the article 'Great Sea Waves', 1934

...the one essential quality of a wave is that it moves; anything that retards or stops its motion dooms it to dissolution and death.

RACHEL CARSON from *The Sea Around Us*, 1951

...the energy in a breaking wave is proportional to the square of its height.

WILLARD BASCOM from *The Crest of the Wave: Adventures in Oceanography*, 1958

Waves are not measured in feet or inches, they are measured in increments of fear.

Surfer **BUZZY TRENT**

There are many kinds of waves in the ocean. They differ greatly in form, velocity, and origin. There are waves too long and low to see that travel on density interfaces below the sea surface. Waves may be raised by ships, or landslides, or the passage of the moon, or earthquakes, or changes in atmospheric pressure. Probably there are kinds of waves that have not yet been discovered. But most waves, and the waves which are most important to mankind, are those raised by the wind.

WILLARD BASCOM from *Waves and Beaches*

...every wave is a masterpiece of originality.

WILLARD BASCOM from *Waves and Beaches*

I don't know who named them swells. There's nothing swell about them. They should have named them awfuls.

HUGO VIHLEN, following his 105-day crossing of the Atlantic in a sloop less than six feet long

As God breathed life into the raw form of Adam, so the wind breathes life into the inert ocean, raises it into a running rhythm, lifts it up out of itself and, finally, transforms the sea into the spectacular glory of breaking waves.

DREW KAMPION from *The Book of Waves, 1989*

Weather

July—stand by,
August—you must
September—you'll remember,
October—all over.

Sailor's rhyme about West Indies hurricanes

Red sky in the morning, sailors take warning,
Red sky at night, sailor's delight.

Mackerel skies and mares' tails
Make tall ships carry short sails.

When the porpoise jumps,
Stand by your pumps.

With the rain before the wind
Stays and topsails you must mind,
But with the wind before the rain
Your topsails you may set again.

If the wind before the rain
Soon you may make sail again.
If the rain before the wind
Shorten sail and halyards mind.

Sea gull, sea gull sit on the sand,
It's never good weather when you're on the land.

> Nautical sayings

Cold's the wind, and wet's the rain,
Saint Hugh be our good speed;
Ill is the weather that bringeth no gain,
Nor helps good hearts in need.

> **THOMAS DEKKER** from *The Shoemakers's Holiday*, 1600

We have had the finest weather imaginable all this day, accompanied
with what is still more agreeable, a fair wind. Heaven that this
favourable gale may continue! for we have had so much of turning to
windward, that the word *helm-a-lee* is become almost as disagreeable to
our ears as the sentence of a judge to a convicted malefactor.

> **BENJAMIN FRANKLIN** from the *Journal of a Voyage*, 1726. Franklin writes of
> his two-and-a-half month crossing from England to America.

This evening the moon being near full, as she rose after eight o'clock,
there appeared a rainbow in a western cloud to windward of us. The
first time I ever saw a rainbow in the night caused by the moon.

> **BENJAMIN FRANKLIN** from the *Journal of a Voyage*, 1726

...nothing in nature is so disagreeable as hard weather at sea...

> **ADMIRAL GEORGE RODNEY,** ca. 1760

All in a hot and copper sky,
The bloody Sun, at noon,
Right up above the mast did stand,
No bigger than the Moon.
Day after day, day after day,
We stuck, nor breath, nor motion;
As idle as a painted ship
Upon a painted ocean.
Water, water, everywhere,
And all the boards did shrink;
Water, water, everywhere,
Nor any drop to drink.

> **SAMUEL TAYLOR COLERIDGE** from the poem 'The Rime of the Ancient
> Mariner', 1798

We had less snow and hail...but we had an abundance of what is worse
to a sailor in cold weather—drenching rain. Snow is blinding, and very
bad when coming upon a coast, but, for genuine discomfort, give me
rain with freezing weather. A snow-storm is exciting, and it does not
wet through the clothes (which is important to a sailor); but a constant
rain there is no escaping from. It wets to the skin, and makes all protec-
tion vain.

> **RICHARD HENRY DANA** from *Two Years Before the Mast*, 1840

When we came up again, which was at four in the morning, it was very
dark, and there was not much wind, but it was raining as I thought I
had never seen it rain before. We had on oilcloth suits and south-wester
caps, and had nothing to do but to stand bolt upright and let it pour
down upon us. There are no umbrellas, and no sheds to go under at sea.

> **RICHARD HENRY DANA** from *Two Years Before the Mast*, 1840. Dana is
> writing about the changing of the watch on board the *Pilgrim* during a storm
> off the California coast.

We are in the doldrums and for six days the ship has rolled horribly in
the swell, with no wind in her sails. The royals and topsails flap drily
against the yards; the ship sways clumsily from side to side against a
background of melancholy noises: straining ropes, grinding braces,
screaming pulley-blocks and distended backstays.

> **HENRI JACQUES**

It always amuses a sailor to observe how little bad weather means to
people who live in towns.

> **MARIN-MARIE** from *Wind Aloft, Wind Alow*, 1947

Wind

...gray-eyed Athene sent them a favorable gale, a fresh West Wind,
singing over the wine-dark sea.

> **HOMER** from *The Odyssey*, ca. 700 BC

...strong winds, the bane of ships, are born of the night.

> **HOMER** from *The Odyssey*, ca. 700 BC

If there is no wind, row.

> Latin proverb

This wind breaketh my heart; that should carry me hence, now stays
me here...

> **SIR WALTER RALEIGH**, 1594

Mildly it kist our sailes, and, fresh and sweet,
As to a stomack sterv'd, whose insides meete,
Meate comes, it came; and swole our sailes...

> **JOHN DONNE** from the poem 'The Storme', 1633

He that at sea prayes for more winde, as well
Under the poles may begge cold, heat in hell.

> **JOHN DONNE** from the poem 'The Calme', 1633

Singing, blow ye winds in the morning,
Blow ye winds high ho!
Clear away your running gear
And blow me bully boys blow!

> English sea chantey 'Blow Ye Winds'

The wind seemed to come with a spite, an edge to it, which threatened
to scrape us off the yards. The mere force of the wind was greater than I
have ever seen it before; but darkness, cold, and wet are the worse parts
of a storm to a sailor.

> **RICHARD HENRY DANA** from *Two Years Before the Mast*, 1840

The wind came blowing blithely from the southwest...and stepped into
the folds of our sail like a winged horse, pulling with a strong and
steady impulse.

> **HENRY DAVID THOREAU** from *Journals*, 1840

Late in the afternoon, for we had lingered long on the island, we raised
our sail for the first time, and for a short hour the southwest wind was
our ally; but it did not please Heaven to abet us long.

> **HENRY DAVID THOREAU** from *A Week on the Concord and Merrimack Rivers*, 1849

To know the laws that govern the winds, and to know that you know
them, will give you an easy mind on your voyage round the world;
otherwise you may tremble at the appearance of every cloud.

> **JOSHUA SLOCUM** from *Sailing Alone Around the World*, 1900

This is the disintegrating power of a great wind: it isolates one from
one's kind.

> **JOSEPH CONRAD** from *Typhoon*, 1903

The wind rules the aspects of the sky and the action of the sea.

> **JOSEPH CONRAD** from *The Mirror of the Sea*, 1906

...it is a gale of wind that makes the sea look old.

> JOSEPH CONRAD from *The Mirror of the Sea*, 1906

There is no part of the world of coasts, continents, oceans, seas, straits, capes, and islands which is not under the sway of a reigning wind...

> JOSEPH CONRAD from *The Mirror of the Sea*, 1906

The breath of God.

> Sailor's description of the wind

Wind is to us what money is to life on shore.

> STERLING HAYDEN from *Wanderer*, 1963

'You must understand that everything, everything at sea depends on the wind.'

> PATRICK O'BRIAN from *HMS Surprise*, 1971. Captain Jack Aubrey is speaking to Dr. Philip Maturin.

Good wind is the gift of God.

> ALAN VILLIERS from *Men Ships and the Sea*, 1973

...I know well enough that I have lost touch with the wind and, in fact, do not like the wind anymore. It jiggles me up, the wind does, and what I really love are windless days, when all is peace. There is a great question in my mind whether a man who is against the wind should longer try to sail a boat.

> E. B. WHITE from 'The Sea and the Wind that Blows', 1977

Women

On Friday morn as we set sail
It was not far from land,
Oh, there I spied a fair pretty maid
With a comb and a glass in her hand.

> Verses to 'The Mermaid', a 16th century Elizabethan sea song

The master, the swabber, the boatswain, and I,
The gunner, and his mate
Lov'd Mall, Meg, and Marian, and Margery,
But none of us car'd for Kate;
For she had a tongue with a tang,
Would cry to a sailor ' Go hang!'
She lov'd not the savour of tar nor of pitch,
Yet a tailor might scratch her where'er she did itch.
Then to sea, boys, and let her go hang!

> **WILLIAM SHAKESPEARE** from *The Tempest*, 1611. Song of Stephano, act II, scene II.

A connection with Women I allow because I cannot prevent it...

> **CAPTAIN JAMES COOK** writing of the attraction of his crew to the women of New Zealand

The parting was very severe. I did not think it would have affected me so much, but I find I love my sweet wench better than I thought.

> **CAPTAIN SAMUEL HOOD** writing about sailing and leaving his wife, ca. 1750

To preserve the ship, therefore, from being pulled to pieces, and the price of refreshments from being raised so high as soon to exhaust our articles of trade, I ordered that no man, except the wooders and waterers, with their guard, should be permitted to go on shore.

> **CAPTAIN SAMUEL WALLIS** describing his difficulties in preserving his ship *Dolphin* due to his crew trading nails for favors from Tahitian women, 1767

In spite of all our precautions, one young woman came aboard onto the poop and stood by one of the hatches above the capstan...the young girl negligently allowed her loincloth to fall to the ground, and appeared to all eyes such as Venus showed herself to the Phrygian shepherd. She had the goddess' celestial form. I ask; how could one keep at work, in the midst of such a spectacle, four hundred Frenchmen, young sailors who for six months had not seen a woman?

> **LOUIS ANTOINE DE BOUGAINVILLE**, French explorer in the South Pacific, writing about an incident in Tahiti, 1768

Cape Cod girls they have no combs,
They comb their hair with codfish bones.

> Cape Cod chantey

This gal she did look good to me,
'Cause I had been ten month at sea.

> Halyard chantey 'Gal With the Blue Dress'

And it's when we come to the old Salthouse Dock,
Them flash little judies to the Pierhead will flock.
The one to the other you'll hear them say:
Oh, here comes young John with his twelve-month pay.

> Capstan chantey 'Goodbye, Fare Ye Well'. The chantey refers to sailors
> returning to Liverpool.

Now when I was a little boy
And so my mother told me,
That if I didn't kiss the gals
Me lips would all grow moldy.
Ye may talk about yer Yankee gals
And round-the-corner Sallies,
But they couldn't make the grade, my boys,
With the girls from down our alley.

> Irish version of the chantey 'Haul Away Joe'

Oh Maggie, Maggie May, they have taken her away,
And never more round Lime Street will she roam.
She's robbed so many sailors and captains of the whalers,
Now poor old Maggie never will come home.

> 19th century Liverpool capstan chantey. It refers to a prostitute named Maggie
> May, who was convicted and sentenced to transportation to the penal colony in
> Botany Bay, Australia. Parts of this same song with somewhat different words
> are also heard on the Beatles album 'Let It Be'; the Beatles were from Liverpool.

Ladies who never walk in the woods, sail over the seas.

HENRY DAVID THOREAU from *Cape Cod*, 1865

Women are jealous of ships. They always suspect the sea. They know they're three of a kind when it comes to a man.

EUGENE O'NEILL from the play *Mourning Becomes Electra*, 1931

A boat to your average woman is just one more damn house to take care of, only it's more uncomfortable, and the man orders her around like Captain Bligh, and she doesn't trust the machinery or the plumbing, and she has to walk six blocks to buy groceries or to get the laundry done.

KURT VONNEGUT from *Wampeters Foma & Granfalloons (Opinions)*, 1965

Work

Anon the master commandeth fast
To his ship-men in all the haste,
To dresse them soon about the mast
   Their takeling to make.

15th century English sea song. This verse is from the oldest known authentic English sea song. Dresse them refers to mustering or lining up for duty.

Six days shalt thou labor and do all thou art able,
And on the seventh—holystone the decks and scrape the cable.

Seaman's traditional 'Philadelphia Catechism', ca. 1830

Down on your knees, boys, holystone the
   decks
Rub'em down, scrub'em down, stiffen out
   your necks.

CHARLES KEELER

We're outward bound for the Bengal Bay.
Get bendin', me lads, it's a hell of a way.

Windlass chantey 'Bold Riley O'

Now, up aloft this yard must go.
We'll haul her free and easy.
Another pull and then belay.
We'll make it all so easy.

> Halyard chantey 'Haul Away for Rosie'

Yachting

He must be adequately well born. He must be a good companion. He must be able to get tight without becoming disagreeable, or he must get tight and go to sleep.

> Informal requirements to avoid being blackballed for membership in The Yacht Club, London, 1815

Yachting may be termed the poetry of the sea. No other sport pastime has been so interwoven with romance and countless memories of daring deeds and achievements.

> **ARTHUR CLARK**, 19th century sea captain and member of the New York Yacht Club

Until you do it all yourself you cannot have any idea of the innumerable minutiae to be attended to in the proper care of a yacht.

> **JOHN MacGREGOR**

If you have to ask what it costs to run a yacht, you can't afford one.

> **J. P. MORGAN**

'Spare no money,' I said... 'Let everything on the *Snark* be of the best... Let the *Snark* be as stanch and strong as any boat afloat. Never mind what it costs to make her stanch and strong; you see that she is stanch and strong and I'll go on writing and earning the money to pay for it.' And I did...as well as I could; for the *Snark* ate up money faster than I could earn it.

> **JACK LONDON** from *The Cruise of the Snark*, 1911. The *Snark*, budgeted at $7,000, eventually cost $30,000.

American yachting needs less common sense, less restrictions, less slide rules, and more sailing.

WILLIAM WASHBURN NUTTING

Yachting history has shown too often that 'progressiveness' is acceptable only if it does not include too much progress.

HOWARD CHAPPELLE

It is a fresh, beautiful, invigorating thing to do, no doubt, to spend a summer on a yacht.

FRANK LESLIE

You may think that the equation is 'boat and water'. It's not. It's 'money and boat'. The water is not really necessary.

ANNIE PROULX from *The Shipping News*

Author Identification

Ackerman, Jennifer 20th century American science writer and educator

Adams, John (1735–1826) American statesman and second U.S. president

Addison, Joseph (1672–1719) English essayist and writer

Alcaeus (ca. 625–575 BC) Greek poet

Angell, Roger (b. 1920) American writer

Ansted, Professor 19th century scientist

Antipater (ca. 120 BC) Greek poet

Aratus (ca. 315–240 BC) Greek poet

Arnold, Matthew (1822–1888) English poet

Ascension, Antonio de la 17th century Spanish monk

Ashley, Clifford (1881–1947) American sailor and author of *The Ashley Book of Knots*

Athenaeus (ca. 200 AD) Greek writer and scholar

Auden, W. H. (1907–1973) English poet

Bacon, Francis (1561–1626) English philosopher and essayist

Bamford, Don 20th century American sailor

Bardiaux, Marcel 20th century French sailor

Barnfield, Richard (1574–1627) English poet

Barr, Charles (1864–1911) Scottish professional yacht captain and one of the greatest racing skippers, who successfully defended the America's Cup three times

Barral, Lieutenant 18th century French mariner

Bascom, Willard (b. 1916) American scientist and oceanographer

Bavier, Bob (b. 1918) American championship racer, America's Cup helmsman in 1964, and publisher of *Yachting* magazine

Beach, Captain Edward L. (b. 1918) American naval officer and writer; commanding officer of the submarine USS *Triton* (SSRN 586) when it circumnavigated the world submerged in 1960

Beattie, John 20th century British sailor

Beston, Henry (1888–1968) American writer

Birtles, Dora (1903–1994) Australian poet, novelist, and travel writer

Bishop, Elizabeth (1911–1979) American poet

Blake, Peter 20th century New Zealand racer and Whitbread competitor

Blake, William (1757–1827) British poet and artist

Bligh, Captain William (1754–1817) English naval officer of mutiny on the *Bounty* notoriety

Blyth, Chay (b. 1940) Scottish sailor and circumnavigator; first to sail around the world nonstop east to west (November 1970–August 1971)

Blythe, George 20th century English cruiser

Bond, Alan (b. 1938) Australian yachtsman and businessman

Borough, William (1530–1598) English captain, navigator, and author of books on navigation

Boswell, James (1740–1795) English writer and biographer

Bougainville, Louis Antoine de (1729–1811) French circumnavigator and Pacific explorer

Bourne, William (active 1565–1588) English gunner, surveyor, and navigator who wrote the first texts in English on navigation and gunnery at sea

Bouvet de Lozier, Jean-Baptiste 18th century French mariner and explorer

Bradford, Gershom (b. 1879) American sailor

Bradford, William (1590–1657) English Pilgrim and American colonist who came to America on the *Mayflower* in 1620; governor of the Plymouth Colony for many years

Brassey, Lady Anna (1839–1887) English travel writer. She made several long voyages with her husband, including a circumnavigation on the yacht *Sunbeam* with her husband, children, servants, and a large crew. She died and was buried at sea.

Brathwaite, Richard (ca. 1588–1673) English poet

Brooks, Fred 20th century American software developer

Brown, Richard (Dick) 19th century American harbor pilot from New York and captain of the yacht *America* in 1851 during the first race in the series which became the America's Cup

Browning, Robert (1812–1889) English poet

Buffett, Jimmy (b. 1946) American singer, songwriter, author and sailor

Burke, Edmund (1729–1797) English political philosopher

Byron, Captain John (1723–1786) English mariner, Pacific explorer, and circumnavigator

Byron, Lord (George Gordon) (1788–1824) English poet

Cabot, Sebastian (ca. 1476–1557) English mapmaker, explorer, and adventurer

Cadamosto, Alvise da (ca. 1432–1488) Portuguese navigator and mariner; sailed for Prince Henry

Calderón de la Barca, Frances (1804–1882) Scottish travel writer

Caligula (12–41 AD) Roman emperor

Callahan, Steve (b. 1952) American sailor who spent 76 days adrift after his sloop sank during a 1982 Atlantic crossing

Camões, Luiz de (ca. 1524–1580) national poet of Portugal and author of *The Lusiads*

Carson, Rachel (1907–1964) American writer and environmentalist

Carteret, Philip (1733–1796) English mariner, circumnavigator, and Pacific explorer

Cavendish, Sir Thomas (1555–1592) English mariner, explorer, and circumnavigator

Cayard, Paul 20th century American world champion sailor, America's Cup competitor, and 1998 Whitbread champion

Champlain, Samuel de (1567–1635) French explorer

Chapman, George (ca. 1559–1634) English poet, playwright, and translator

Chappelle, Howard (1901–1975) American maritime historian, museum curator, and writer

Chaucer, Geoffrey (ca. 1343–1400) English poet and author of the *Canterbury Tales*

Cherry-Garrard, Apsley (1886–1959) English zoologist and Antarctic explorer; survivor of Scott's ill-fated Antarctic polar expedition of 1912

Chichester, Sir Francis (1901–1972) English yachtsman and circumnavigator

Chiles, Webb 20th century American circumnavigator and author

Chopin, Kate (1851–1904) American writer

Clark, Arthur (1841–1922) American insurance executive, yachtsman, and yachting historian

Coleridge, Samuel Taylor (1772–1834) English poet

Colgate, Steve 20th century American sailor and sail educator

Columbus, Christopher (1451–1506) Italian mariner and discoverer of America

Conner, Dennis (b. 1942) American world champion racer and four-time winner of the America's Cup

Conrad, Joseph (1857–1924) English novelist and mariner

Cook, Captain James (1728–1779) English mariner, naval officer, and Pacific ocean explorer

Cooper, James Fenimore (1789–1851) American writer

Cordes, Simon de 16th century Dutch mariner and explorer

Cortes, Martin (1532–1589) Spanish geographer; author of *Breve Compendio de la Arte de Navegar* (1561)

Cosens, William 19th century master of *Euterpe*, a British East Indiaman

Cowper, William (1731–1800) English poet

Crane, Hart (1899–1932) American poet

Crane, Stephen (1871–1900) American writer

Culler, R. D. 'Pete' (1910–1978) American boatbuilder

Dalrymple, Alexander (1737–1808) English chartmaker and first hydrographer to the Navy (1795)

Dampier, William (1652–1715) English navigator, mariner, and Pacific explorer

Dana, Richard Henry (1815–1882) American mariner and writer

Dante Alighieri (1265–1321) Italian poet and author of the *The Divine Comedy*

Darwin, Charles (1809–1882) English naturalist and scientific theorist; author of *The Origin of Species* (1859)

Dashew, Steve 20th century American sailor

Davis, Charles G. (1870–1959) American ship model builder and historian

Davis, John (ca. 1550–1605) English mariner, explorer, circumnavigator, developer of navigational instruments, and author of *The Seamans Secrets*

Davison, Ann 20th century English sailor and writer; first woman to cross the Atlantic singlehanded

Day, George (b. 1950) American sailor and writer

Day, Thomas Fleming (1861–1919) American yacht designer, nautical journalist, and editor of *The Rudder*

Decatur, Stephen (1779–1820) American naval officer

Defoe, Daniel (1660–1731) English novelist and journalist; author of *Robinson Crusoe*

Degnon, Dom 20th century American sailor

Deighton, Len (b. 1929) English writer

Dekker, Thomas (ca. 1570–1632) English playwright and dramatist

Dey, Richard Morris 20th century American educator and writer

Dickens, Charles (1812–1870) English novelist

Dickinson, Emily (1830–1886) American poet

Dickson, Chris 20th century New Zealand sailor and America's Cup competitor

Diebitsch, Captain (d. 1957) captain of barque *Pamir* when she sank in a hurricane in 1957; perished with most of the crew

Dinesen, Isak (Karen Blixen) (1885–1962) Danish writer; author of *Out of Africa* (1937)

Doctorow, E. L. (b. 1931) American novelist and educator

Donne, John (ca. 1572–1631) English poet

Dos Passos, John (1896–1970) American novelist

Drake, Sir Francis (ca. 1540–1596) English mariner, adventurer, and circumnavigator (1577–80)

Drake, Tom (1863–1936) English singlehander who disappeared in the Pacific in 1936

Dumas, Vito (1900–1965) Argentinian singlehand sailor and circumnavigator; first to sail around the world via Cape Horn by going east to west

Duncan, Roger 20th century American sailor and author of cruising guides

Dunraven, Lord (Windham-Quin, Wyndham Thomas) (b. 1841) English nobleman and America's Cup competitor in 1893 and 1895

Earle, Sylvia 20th century American oceanographer, explorer, and diver

Eliot, T. S. (1888–1965) American poet and playwright

Ellis, Thomas 16th century English mariner who sailed with Martin Frobisher on his third voyage in search of a northwest passage and wrote an account of the trip

Emerson, Ralph Waldo (1803–1882) American philosopher and writer who sailed from Boston to Liverpool on the packet-ship *Washington Irving* in 1847

Euripides (ca. 485–406 BC) Greek playwright

Evelyn, John (1620–1706) English author and diarist

Faber, Felix 15th century monk, philosopher, and theologian

Falconer, William, 18th century author

Fehlman, Pierre 20th century Swiss mariner

Field, Ross 20th century New Zealand racer and Whitbread competitor

Fielding, Henry (1707–1754) English author

Florio, John (ca. 1553–1625) English translator and lexicographer

Fournier, Georges 17th century French philosopher

Fowles, John (b. 1926) English author

Franklin, Benjamin (1706–1790) American diplomat, publisher, and inventor

Frobisher, Sir Martin (1535–1594) English navigator and explorer who made voyages to discover a northwest passage

Garcie, Pierre (ca. 1435–1520) French pilot who created in the 1480s what is very likely the first printed rutter

Gardner, John (1933–1982) American writer, scholar, and educator

Garrick, David (1717–1779) English actor and theater manager

Gau, Jean (b. 1902) French sailor and circumnavigator

Gerbault, Alain (1896–1941) French circumnavigator, author, and tennis player

Gibbon, Edward (1737–1794) English historian

Gibbons, Thomas (1757–1826) American lawyer, politician, and steamboat operator

Gilbert, Sir Humphrey (ca. 1539–1583) English navigator; lost at sea

Graham, R. D. early 20th century English naval officer and sailor

Graham, Robin Lee (b. 1949) American circumnavigator. At the age of 16 he departed Los Angeles on a five-year circumnavigation and became the youngest person to make the voyage.

Grahame, Kenneth (1859–1932) English writer

Greeley, Horace (1811–1872) American journalist

Griffiths, Maurice (b. 1902) English yacht designer and author

Hakluyt, Richard (ca. 1552–1616) English historian and travel writer

Hall, Christopher 16th century English master of the bark *Gabriel* during the first of Martin Frobisher's three voyages to America in search of the northwest passage

Hardy, Thomas (1840–1928) English novelist

Hawkesworth, John (ca. 1715–1773) English writer

Hayden, Sterling (1916–1986) American sailor, actor and author

Hayes, Captain Edward 16th century English mariner and captain of the *Golden Hinde* in 1583

Heath, Edward (b. 1916) English sailor, racer, and Prime Minister

Hemingway, Ernest (1898–1961) American writer

Herbert, George (1593–1633) English poet

Herreshoff, L. Francis (1890–1972) American naval architect and sailor

Herreshoff, Nathanael G. (1848–1938) American naval architect and yacht designer who was known as the Wizard of Bristol; he designed six yachts which successfully defended the America's Cup from 1893 to 1920.

Herrick, Robert (1591–1674) English poet and cleric

Hesiod (8th century BC) Greek poet

Hildebrand, Arthur Sturgis (1887–1924) American cruiser and nautical writer; lost at sea

Hiscock, Eric (1908–1986) English cruiser, writer, and circumnavigator; sailed with wife Susan on a series of boats named *Wanderer*

Holmes, Oliver Wendell (1809–1894) American physician and writer

Homer (8th century BC) Greek poet

Hood, Captain Samuel (1724–1816) English naval officer and admiral

Horace (Quintus Horatius Flaccus) (65–8 BC) Roman poet

Howell, Bill 'Tahiti' (b. 1927) Australian catamaran sailor and racer

Hoyt, Garry 20th century American yacht designer

Hudson, Henry (d. 1611) English navigator and explorer of North America

Hughes, Richard (1900–1976) English writer

Huntington, Anna Seaton American 1992 Olympic bronze medalist in women's pair rowing and member of the 1995 America^3 women's team in the America's Cup

Innes, Hammond (1913–1998) Scottish author, sailor, and travel writer

James, Naomi (b. 1948) New Zealand sailor; first woman to sail single-handed around the world, September 1977–June 1978

Janes, John 16th century Englishman who sailed with Captain John Davis on Davis' voyage in 1585 to search for a northwest passage

Jewett, Sarah Orne (1849–1909) American writer

Jobson, Gary 20th century American sailor, tactician, and America's Cup competitor

Johnson, Irving (1905–1990) American mariner and writer

Johnson, Samuel (1709–1784) English author and lexicographer

Jones, John Paul (1747–1792) American naval officer and mariner

Jones, Tristan (1924–1995) English sailor and author

Kampion, Drew 20th century American surfer and journalist

Keats, John (1795–1821) English poet

Keeler, Charles (1871–1937) American sailor, author, and museum director

Kennedy, John F. (1917–1963) American politician, 35th president of the United States (1961–1963)

Keppel, Rear Admiral Augustus (1725–1786) English naval officer; made First Lord of the Admiralty in 1782

Kidder, Tracy 20th century American writer and Pulitzer Prize winner

Kilroy, John B. 'Jim' 20th century American yachtsman and maxi-racer

King, R. 'Bunty' 20th century American sailor

Kipling, Rudyard (1865–1936) English novelist and poet

Knight, Kathryn Lasky 20th century American sailor and writer

Knox-Johnston, Robin (b. 1939) English sailor and circumnavigator who won the first solo, nonstop, round-the-world race, 1968–1969

Koch, William 20th century American yachtsman and energy company executive

Kolius, John 20th century American racer and America's Cup competitor

Kulczycki, Chris 20th century American sailor and journalist

Kunhardt, Charles P. (ca. 1848–1889) American yachting journalist

Kurth, Rear Admiral Ronald J. (b. 1931) American naval officer

Kyle, John 19th century sailing master

Lao-tzu (6th century BC) Chinese philosopher and founder of Taoism

Le Carré, John (b. 1931) English author

Le Toumelin, Jacques-Yves (b. 1920) French sailor

Leonidas of Tarentum (ca. 290–220 BC) Greek poet and epigrammatist

Leslie, Frank (1821–1880) American publisher and journalist

Lethbridge, T.C. 20th century English maritime author and historian

Lewis, Perry (1884–1957) British writer

Lexcen, Ben (1936–1988) Australian yacht designer and innovator of the winged keel which helped *Australia II* win the America's Cup in 1983

Li Po (701–762) Chinese poet

Lindbergh, Anne Morrow (b. 1906) American author, poet, and aviator

Lipton, Sir Thomas (1850–1931) Scottish businessman, tea merchant, and yachtsman who challenged unsuccessfully for the America's Cup five times from 1899 to 1930

London, Jack (1876–1916) American writer and seaman

Long, Huey 20th century American yachtsman and maxi-racer

Longfellow, Henry Wadsworth (1807–1882) American poet

Loomis, Alfred (1890–1968) American sailor, nautical journalist, and author

Lowell, James Russell (1819–1891) American poet

Lowell, Robert (1917–1977) American poet

Lozier, Jean-Baptiste Bouvet de (1705–1788) French sailor and Antarctic explorer

Lucian of Samothrace (ca. 115–181 AD) Greek essayist and writer

Lucretius (Titus Lucretius Carus) (99–55 BC) Roman poet and philosopher

M'Quahe, Peter 19th century English naval officer

MacGregor, John (1825–1892) Scottish writer and sailor

Magellan, Ferdinand (ca. 1480–1521) Portuguese explorer and mariner who led the first circumnavigation of the globe (1519–1522)

Mahan, Alfred Thayer (1840–1914) American naval officer, theorist, and historian

Manry, Robert (b. 1918) American journalist and sailor. In 1965 he crossed the Atlantic from the United States to England in *Tinkerbelle*, a 13.5-foot sloop, at that time the smallest sailboat to successfully make the voyage.

Marin-Marie (Marin-Marie Durand Couppel de St. Front) 20th century French artist and cruiser

Martin, Evelyn George (1881–1945) English sailor and cruiser

Martyr, Weston (b. 1885) English sailor and author

Masefield, John (1878–1967) English mariner and poet; poet laureate (1930–1967)

Mason, Arthur (1876–1955) American sailor

Maury, Matthew Fontaine (1806–1873) American naval officer and oceanographer

Maury, Richard 20th century American cruiser

McMullen, Richard T. (1830–1891) English sailor and early promoter of singlehanded sailing

Medina, Pedro de (ca. 1493–1567) Spanish writer on navigation; wrote *Arte de Navegar*, published in 1545

Melges, Buddy (b. 1930) American racer, world championship sailor, Olympic Gold Medalist (Solings, 1972), boat designer, and America's Cup helmsman in 1992

Melville, Herman (1819–1891) American writer, author of *Moby Dick* (1851)

Miles, Alfred Hart (1883–1956) composer of 'Anchors Aweigh'

Mitchell, Carleton (b. 1910) American sailor and author

Mohlhenrich, Janice 20th century American sailor and racer

Moitessier, Bernard (1925–1994) French circumnavigator and small boat sailor

Monsarrat, Nicholas (1910–1979) English novelist and author of *The Cruel Sea* (1951)

Monson, Sir William (1568–1643) English naval officer; author of *Naval Tracts*

Moore, Jim 20th century American cruiser

Moore, Marianne (1887–1972) American poet

Morgan, J. P. (1837–1913) American financier and philanthropist

Morison, Samuel Eliot (1887–1976) American historian, author, and naval officer

Mosbacher, Emil 'Bus' (b. 1922) American yachtsman and America's Cup competitor

Murnan, Bill 20th century American sailor and circumnavigator

Newton, Sir Isaac (1642–1727) English mathematician and physicist

Nicholson, Charles 20th century British yacht and J-boat designer

Nimitz, Chester W. (1885–1966) American naval officer and World War II fleet admiral

Norman, Geoffrey 20th century American journalist

Norman, Robert 16th century navigator, maker of navigational instruments, and author of navigational texts

Novak, Skip 20th century sailor and Whitbread competitor

Nutting, William Washburn (1884–1924) American sailor, nautical journalist and editor; founder of the Cruising Club of America; lost at sea

O'Brian, Patrick (b. 1914) English author and creator of the Aubrey/Maturin novels

O'Brien, Conor (1880–1952) Irish sailor and author; first to circumnavigate (1922–25) by going south of Cape Horn, Cape of Good Hope, and Cape Leeuwin off Australia

O'Neill, Eugene (1888–1953) American playwright

Olson, Charles (1910–1970) American poet

Olsson, Magnus 20th century ocean racer

Osorio, Jeronymo (1506–1580) Portuguese historian and bishop of Sylves

Packer, Sir Frank 20th century Australian sailor, publisher, and media magnate. In 1962 he led the first Australian challenge for the America's Cup.

Palley, Reese 20th century American sailor

Pardey, Larry 20th century American sailor and cruiser

Pardey, Lin 20th century American sailor and cruiser

Payne, Bob 20th century American sailor and cruiser

Payson, Herb 20th century American sailor and cruiser

Penn, William (1644–1718) American political leader and founder of Pennsylvania

Pepys, Samuel (1633–1703) English diarist and naval administrator

Pericles (ca. 495–429 BC) Athenian statesman

Petty, Sir William (1623–1687) English political economist and inventor of the catamaran

Pflugk, H. A. V. von 20th century merchant marine captain

Piailug, Mau 20th century Caroline Islander and traditional navigator

Pierce, Eben 19th century American sailor who gave *Spray* to Joshua Slocum

Pigafetta, Antonio (ca. 1491–1535) Venetian nobleman who completed Magellan's circumnavigation

Pillsbury, John (1846–1919) Gulf Stream explorer and American oceanographer

Pindar (ca. 522–438 BC) Greek lyric poet

Plautus, Titus Maccius (ca. 254–184 BC) Roman playwright

Pliny the Elder (Gaius Plinius Secundus) (ca. 23–79 AD) Roman writer

Poe, Edgar Allan (1809–1849) American author and poet

Poole, John (1786–1872) English playwright

Porter, Captain David (1780–1843) American naval officer who raided the British whaling fleet in the Pacific in 1813

Pratt, Alby 20th century Australian racer and Whitbread competitor

Prime, Alanson J. 19th century American yachtsman and first president of the New York Yacht Racing Association

Propertius, Sextus (ca. 50–15 BC) Roman poet

Prothero, Robert 20th century American boatbuilder at Port Townsend, Washington

Proulx, Annie (b. 1935) American writer

Publilius, Syrus (ca. 50–15 BC) Roman writer

Purchas, Samuel (ca. 1577–1626) English priest and problematic editor of some accounts of early voyages and explorations; editor of *Purchas His Pilgrimes* (1625)

Pye, Peter (1902–1966) English sailor and physician

Queiros, Pedro de (1565–1615) Portuguese navigator, mariner, and Pacific explorer

Raban, Jonathan (b. 1942) English author and travel writer

Raleigh, Sir Walter (1554–1618) English adventurer, navigator and historian

Ray, John (1627–1705) English naturalist and botanist; inventor of the concept of species and pioneer in development of a system to classify plants and animals

Riesenberg, Felix (1879–1939) American mariner and author

Robinson, William A. (b. 1904) American circumnavigator, writer, and shipyard operator

Rodger, N. A. M. (b. 1949) English naval historian and author

Rodney, Admiral George (1718–1792) English naval officer, admiral, and fleet commander

Ross, James Clark (1800–1862) Scottish naval officer, circumnavigator, and Arctic and Antarctic magnetic surveyor

Rossetti, Christina (1830–1894) English poet

Rossetti, Dante Gabriel (1828–1882) English poet and painter

Ruskin, John (1819–1900) English essayist, critic and reformer

Russell, John (b. 1885) British sailor

Saadi (Sheikh Muslih-uddin Saadi Shirazi) (ca. 1213–1292) Persian poet

Salter, James (b. 1925) American author

Sanchez, Thomas 20th century American writer

Sandburg, Carl (1878–1967) American poet

Saumarez, Philip (1710–1747) English naval officer who sailed with Anson on his circumnavigation; eventually succeeded to second in command of the expedition

Sayers, Dorothy L. (1893–1957) English writer

Schouten, Willem (ca. 1567–1625) Dutch mariner, explorer, and discoverer of the Drake Passage at Cape Horn

Seneca, Lucius Annaeus the Younger (ca. 4 BC–65 AD) Roman philosopher and poet

Settle, Dionise 16th century English sailor and master of the ship *Aide* during Martin Frobisher's second voyage to America to look for the Northwest Passage, 1577

Sexton, Anne (1928–1974) American poet

Shacochis, Bob 20th century American writer

Shakespeare, William (1564–1616) English playwright and poet

Shaw, George Bernard (1856–1950) English playwright and novelist

Shelley, Percy Bysshe (1792–1822) English poet

Slocum, Joshua (1844–1910) Canadian mariner and writer; first to circumnavigate single-handed; lost at sea

Smeeton, Miles (1906–1988) English army officer, sailor, and circumnavigator

Smith, Adam (1723–1790) Scottish political economist and philosopher

Smith, Captain John (ca. 1580–1631) English explorer, soldier, and founder of the Virginia colony in 1607

Smith, Hervey Garrett 20th century American maritime illustrator and writer

Sophocles (ca. 496–405 BC) Greek playwright

Spavens, William 18th century English writer; author of *The Seaman's Narrative* (1796)

Sperry, Willard L. (1882–1954) American Protestant clergyman and theologian

Stephens, Olin James (b. 1908) American naval architect and designer of six America's Cup winners; co-founder of the design firm of Sparkman & Stephens

Stephens, Roderick (1909–1995) American naval architect and America's Cup competitor

Stevens, Thomas 16th century Englishman

Stevenson, Robert Louis (1850–1894) Scottish novelist; author of *Treasure Island* (1883) and *Kidnapped* (1886)

Stokes, Francis 20th century American sailor and single-hander

Stone, Robert 20th century American writer

Sullivan, Sir Edward (1852–1928) English yachtsman

Swinburne, Algernon Charles (1837–1909) English poet and novelist

Synesius (5th century AD) Greek merchant

Synge, John Millington (1871–1909) Irish playwright

Taylor, Roger C. 20th century American sailor

Tennyson, Alfred, Lord (1809–1892) English poet; poet laureate (1850–1892)

Tetley, Nigel (b. 1924) English trimaran sailor and circumnavigator

Thomas, Dylan (1914–1953) Welsh poet

Thoreau, Henry David (1817–1862) American author and philosopher

Thucydides (ca. 460–400 BC) Greek historian and writer

Tilman, H. W. (1898–1977) English mountaineer, sailor and writer

Tolkien, J.R.R. (1892–1973) English writer

Tomlinson, H.M. (1873–1958) English novelist and journalist

Tompkins, Warwick M. 20th century American mariner

Trent, Buzzy 20th century American surfer

Trollope, Anthony (1815–1882) English novelist; author of the Palliser novels

Turner, Ted (b. 1938) American television executive, yachtsman and successful America's Cup defender on *Courageous*, 1977

Twain, Mark (1835–1910) American humorist, author, and traveler

Valentijn, Johan 20th century naval architect and America's Cup designer

Van de Weile, Annie 20th century Belgian sailor and circumnavigator

Vanderbilt, Harold 'Mike' (1884–1970) American businessman, yachtsman, and three-time successful defender of the America's Cup

Vigor, John 20th century American sailor

Vihlen, Hugo (b. 1931) holds the record for the smallest sailboat crossing of the North Atlantic; he sailed a boat only 5'4" long, in 1992.

Villiers, Alan (1903–1982) Australian mariner and author

Virgil (Publius Vergilius Maro) (70–19 BC) Roman poet

Vitry, Jacques de (1170–1240) French bishop and historian

Vonnegut, Kurt (b. 1922) American author

Walker, Ronald (1909–1929) Australian reporter and sailor

Walker, Stuart H. 20th century American sailor, author, and journalist

Wallis, Samuel (1728–1795) English naval officer, mariner, and South Pacific explorer; first European to arrive in Tahiti

Walter, Richard (ca. 1716–1785) English naval chaplain who sailed with George Anson on *Centurion* for much of Anson's circumnavigation; he left the voyage at Macao.

Walters, Angus 20th century Canadian captain of the schooner *Bluenose*

Weert, Sebald de 16th century Dutch mariner and explorer

Westheimer, Dr. Ruth 20th century American writer and television personality

Wharram, Jim (b. 1928) English sailor and designer

Wheeler, Captain Edward 18th century English naval officer

White, E. B. (1899–1985) American writer, essayist, and sailor

Whitemarsh, R. P. 20th century American naval officer

Whiting, William (1825–1878) American composer

Whitman, Walt (1819–1892) American poet and journalist; author of *Leaves of Grass*
Wicker, Tom (b. 1926) American writer and journalist
Woolf, Virginia (1882–1941) English writer and essayist
Wordsworth, William (1770–1850) English poet, poet laureate (1843–1850)
Worsley, F. A. (1872–1943) English Antarctic explorer
Worthington, Kimo 20th century ocean racer
Xenophon (ca. 431–352 BC) Greek historian, soldier, and essayist
Young, Filson (1876–1938) English journalist and naval officer

Originator Index

Keyword Index

Permissions

Jennifer Ackerman, from 'When the Sea Calls'. Copyright © 1997 by Jennifer Ackerman. Reprinted by permission of Jennifer Ackerman.

Roger Angell, from 'Ancient Mariner' from The New Yorker. Copyright © 1993 by Roger Angell. Reprinted by permission of Roger Angell.

Don Bamford, from the article 'Getting off the Ground'. Reprinted by permission of *Cruising World* magazine.

Willard Bascom, from *Waves and Beaches: The Dynamics of the Ocean Surface*. Copyright © 1964 by Willard Bascom. Reprinted by permission of Bantam Doubleday Dell.

Bob Bavier, from *Sailing to Win*. Copyright © 1983 by Bob Bavier. Reprinted by permission of Bob Bavier.

Henry Beston, from *The Outermost House*. Copyright © 1928, 1949, 1956 by Henry Beston. Copyright © 1977 by Elizabeth C. Beston. Reprinted by permission of Henry Holt and Company, Inc.

Jimmy Buffett, from *A Pirate Looks at Fifty*. Copyright © 1998 by Jimmy Buffett. Reprinted by permission of Random House, Inc.

John le Carré, from *The Secret Pilgrim*. Copyright © 1991 by John le Carré. Reprinted by permission of Random House, Inc.

Rachel Carson, from *The Sea Around Us*. Copyright © 1950, 1951, 1961 by Rachel Carson, renewed 1979 by Roger Christie. Reprinted by permission of Oxford University Press, Inc.

Lionel Casson, from *Ships and Seafaring in Ancient Times*. Copyright © 1994. Reprinted by permission of the University of Texas Press.

Steve Colgate, from the article 'The Stages of Heavy Weather Sailing'. Reprinted by permission of *Sail* magazine.

Dennis Conner, *Comeback: My Race for the America's Cup* by Dennis Conner with Bruce Stannard. Copyright © 1987 by Dennis Conner Sports, Inc. Reprinted by permission of Dennis Conner Sports, Inc.

Anne Davison, from the article 'Hall of Fame'. Reprinted by permission of *Cruising World* magazine.

George Day, from the editorial 'The Wide Pacific'. Reprinted by permission of *Cruising World* magazine.

Dom Degnon, from *Sails Full and By*. Copyright © 1995 by Dom Degnon. Reprinted by permission of Sheridan House, Inc.

E.L. Doctorow, from *Billy Bathgate*. Copyright © 1989 by E.L. Doctorow. Reprinted by permission of Random House, Inc.

T.S. Eliot. Excerpt from "The Dry Salvages" in *Four Quartets*, copyright © 1943 by T.S. Eliot and renewed 1971 by Esme Valerie Eliot. Reprinted by permission of Harcourt Brace & Company.